A TREATISE

ON THE

HISTORY OF CONFESSION

A TREATISE

ON THE

HISTORY OF CONFESSION

UNTIL IT DEVELOPED INTO

AURICULAR CONFESSION

A.D. 1215

BY

C. M. ROBERTS, B.D.,

RECTOR OF ALDRIDGE, STAFFORDSHIRE;
SOMETIME SCHOLAR OF S. JOHN'S COLLEGE, CAMBRIDGE;
HEAD MMSTER OF MONMOUTH SCHOOL 1859—1891;
RECTOR OF BRINKLEY, CAMBRIDGESHIRE, 1889—1893.

LONDON:
C. J. CLAY AND SONS,
CAMBRIDGE UNIVERSITY PRESS WAREHOUSE,
AVE MARIA LANE.

1901

CAMBRIDGE UNIVERSITY PRESS
Cambridge, New York, Melbourne, Madrid, Cape Town,
Singapore, São Paulo, Delhi, Mexico City

Cambridge University Press
The Edinburgh Building, Cambridge CB2 8RU, UK

Published in the United States of America by Cambridge University Press, New York

www.cambridge.org
Information on this title: www.cambridge.org/9781107620322

First published 1901
First paperback edition 2013

A catalogue record for this publication is available from the British Library

ISBN 978-1-107-62032-2 Paperback

PREFACE.

TO my brethren, the Clergy and lay-members of the Christian Church,

I offer this Treatise on the History of Confession in the hope that, by following the sequence of the authorities in the Church, they may gain a more sure and correct knowledge of the doctrine of Confession as to the occasion of its practice during the first twelve centuries and to the lack of any necessity during that period of revealing to a Priest all the evil thoughts and lesser sins, of which a member of the society of Christians may have been guilty.

I have endeavoured to put forward facts of history rather than theories, based upon the teaching of the Church which gained ascendancy in subsequent ages.

I have carefully verified all the passages put forward except the few marked with an asterisk.

I know not of any other Treatise on this subject, in which the chronological order of authorities has been so carefully observed.

With the earnest desire that these pages may be the means of giving assistance to some who approach this subject with an open mind, I send forth the result of the labour of many months, with the hope that truth may thereby be advanced.

C. M. R.

LIST OF BOOKS REFERRED TO.

Bellarmine. Paris, 1608.
Bingham. London, 1726.
Browne, Bp. XXXIX Articles. 1856.
Canones. 2nd Council of Chalons.
    ,,   Conc. Laodiceni. Beveridge, 1672.
Chrysostom. Trans. by H. Hollier. London.
Clemens of Alexandria, per J. Potter. Oxf. 1715.
Cotelerius. Apostolic Fathers and Constitutions. Amsterd. 1724.
Cyprian. Joannes le Preux. 1593.
    ,,   Trans. by N. Marshall. London, 1717.
Damiani, P. Ed. Cajetan. 1663.
Ellicott, Bp. Bible Commentary. Cassell, 1897.
Eusebius. Ed. E. Burton. Oxf. 1856.
Green. Short Hist. of England.
Homilies. S.P.C.K.
Hook, Dean. The Church and her Ordinances. 1876.
Hooker. Eccles. Polity. S. Walton. Oxf. 1793.
Hunt. Eng. Church of Middle Ages. 1895.
Lea, Dr H. C. Auricular Confession and Indulgences. 1896.
Marshall, N. Penitential Discipline. A. C. Theo. Parker, 1844.
Martene. De antiq. Eccles. Ritibus. Antw. 1736.
Maskell, W. Absolution. 1849.
    ,,   Anc. Liturgy of Ch. of Eng. 3 edit. 1882.
Migne. Various Eccles. Writers. Paris, 1845—1857.
Morinus. Comment. Hist. de Discip. Paris, 1651.
Origen. Paris, 1512.
Palmer, W. English Ritual. 1845.

Pusey, E.   Adv. on hearing Confession.   Gaume, 1878.
  ,,   Notes on Tertullian.   Lib. Fathers.   Oxf. 1842.
Robertson.   History of Christian Church.   1858.
Salisbury, Bp.   Pastoral Letter.   1898.
Smith's Dict. of Christian Antiq. (exomologesis).
Sozomen.   Eccles. Hist.   Hussey.   Oxf. 1860.
Spence, Dean.   Ch. of Eng. for People.   Cassell, 1896.
Swete, Prof.   Services and Service Books.   1896.
Tertullian.   Leips. 1839.
Thorpe.   Anc. Laws and Institutes of Eng.   1840.
Wake, Archbp.   Trans. of Apostolic Fathers.   3 edit.   London,
    1719.
Wakeman, H. O.   Ch. of England.   1897.
Wheatly, C.   Common Prayer.   Bohn, 1853.

CHAPTER I.

AURICULAR Confession or Sacramental Confession is understood to be private Confession to a Priest of all sins and the circumstances, occasions and inducements of them, with a view of receiving Absolution from him, acting with priestly power and authority : and to be necessary to salvation and of divine right.

I shall endeavour simply to trace the customs and the powers of the Christian Church as to the Confession of its members, from its first establishment as recorded in Holy Scripture, through the various changes of succeeding ages, which finally developed into Auricular Confession, imposed on all Christians and practised and retained by those who are in communion with the Church of Rome, but afterwards rejected by the Reformers of the English Church on the ground of not being "of divine right and command necessary."

Before entering upon the different phases of Confession itself, I will try to clear the way upon a few important matters.

It is well known that our Saviour, while on earth, built up ordinances of the Christian Church on what was familiar among the Jews, and in the regular usage of the Jewish Church.

As Baptism and the Lord's Supper were instituted on usages of the Jews in their outward form; and an inward spiritual grace was attached by our Lord to these Sacraments, so it may be that the discipline of the members of Christ's Church was to be enforced by cutting off notorious offenders from the privileges of the Church after the same manner as the Jews controlled their members by Excommunication of different grades of severity. A Jew then in our Lord's time, would well understand the use of such expressions as 'binding and loosing'; and also of being as 'a heathen or a publican.'

Now in the Gospel of S. Matthew[1] we read that after Simon Peter had stated his belief saying, "Thou art the Christ, the Son of the living God," our Lord conferred on S. Peter a certain very strong power in the following words: "I will give unto thee the keys of the kingdom of heaven; and whatsoever thou shalt bind on earth shall be bound in heaven: and whatsoever thou shalt loose on earth shall be loosed in heaven."

Now what would a Jew of those days conclude as to the power conferred on S. Peter? Would he not naturally lead his thoughts to the binding and loosing in some grade of Excommunication, which from his youth he knew to be the means, adopted in the Church of his fathers, to deter offenders from breaking the Law and the Commandments of God? Thus a man was held in the bondage of his sin or released therefrom with an authority, which would be upheld in heaven itself.

Some outward form of government was necessary for the well-being of the Church, as a Society. Members

[1] S. Matt. xvi. 19.

were admitted through Baptism, and were incorporated as members of Christ, children of God and inheritors of the kingdom of heaven. But as members may fall into gross sin after they have been admitted into Christ's Church, it is necessary that they no longer should be allowed to participate in the privileges of the Church, as long as they continue in that sin or show no desire to free themselves from the entanglements of it, and that they be cut off from communion or excommunicated until such time as they confess their sin, make promises of amendment in their life and seek reconciliation. By their sin they not only deserve the wrath of God, but they bring a scandal upon the community, in which they have been enrolled. All sin is certainly a sin against God, but at the same time it also involves an offence against the society, to which the sinner belongs, or against an individual who has been wronged. Such a sinner against the Church or against his neighbour may after sorrow expressed and reparation made be absolved or freed from the censure under which he had fallen, and be restored to the privileges he had forfeited.

In the Jewish Temple worship the ministry of the Priest was very considerable towards the forgiveness of sins.

[1] The man that sins in concealing his knowledge hearing the voice of swearing or in touching an unclean thing or in uttering an oath " when he shall be guilty in one of these things, shall confess that he hath sinned in that thing...and the priest shall make an atonement for him concerning his sin...and the priest shall make an atonement for him for his sin which he hath sinned, and

---

[1] Lev. v. 1—10.

it shall be forgiven him." The offender should confess
his guilt and provide at his own cost a sacrifice for the
Priest to offer. Here it is evident that under the Jewish
covenant, the chief action which showed that a sinner
was truly penitent for the sin that he had committed
or that he had been partaker of, by concealing his knowledge of it, was to make a formal acknowledgment of
such transgression and to offer up a sacrifice for his sin
at his own cost. Other outward acts were also regarded
as worthy signs of sorrow for sin.

The Ninevites appeared in sackcloth and ashes for
their wrong-doing, and their prayer was heard.

And from those sentences of Holy Scripture, taken
from the Psalms and Prophets, in our Book of Service
appointed to be used at Morning and Evening Prayer,
as a preparation of our minds before taking part in the
General Confession, we trace directions to set our heart
right before God, rather than to rely upon any formal
act to gain pardon of our sins.

We may by a thoughtful study of our Lord's directions and teaching throughout His ministry, as recorded
by the Evangelists, see that He sets aside the old formalism
of the Jews for a good and spiritual life, that we should
seek by prayer assistance of the Spirit of God, whereby
our hearts may be inclined towards the will of God, so
that we abhor that which is evil, shrink from sin, and
rely upon the merits of the sacrifice of Christ, as
sufficient to atone for our sins and those of the whole
world.

Our Saviour during His earthly ministry, informs
His Apostles that He had been sent into the world by
the Father to redeem mankind, and that, to this end, He

had the full co-operation of the Holy Spirit : that He had complete knowledge of the will of God and carried it out in every particular, for the Spirit was given Him without measure.

He shows by act and deed that He could perform miracles at will and knew the hearts of men, and what was in them. He tells His followers, whom He appointed to the ministry, "as my Father sent me even so send I you." They were appointed by Christ to turn men from their evil ways and to lead them into the way of salvation : they should have an ever-increasing but some-what limited knowledge of the will of their Heavenly Father, and they would by prayer obtain the necessary aid of the Holy Spirit, though such inspirations would be only occasional and these bounded by circumstances. They were endowed with a portion of miraculous power and we have instances of their insight into the secret thoughts of men's minds, made known to us.

Then again they sent others to bring men within the fold of Christ's Church but with limitations to their privileges and powers, and yet with sufficient to control and direct the working of the Church for the eternal welfare of those who would be guided by her.

After S. Peter's Confession[1] "Thou art the Christ, the Son of the living God" our Saviour answered and said unto him, " Blessed art thou, Simon Barjona, for flesh and blood hath not revealed it unto thee, but my Father which is in heaven. And I say unto thee, That thou art Peter, and upon this rock I will build my Church, and the gates of hell shall not prevail against it. And I will give thee the keys of the kingdom of heaven :

[1] S. Matt. xvi. 16—19.

and whatsoever thou shalt bind on earth shall be bound in heaven, and whatsoever thou shalt loose on earth shall be loosed in heaven."

Our Saviour further gives direction of the course to be pursued when a brother had committed a trespass against another[1], "Go and tell him his fault between thee and him alone : if he shall hear thee, thou hast gained thy brother. But if he will not hear thee, then take with thee one or two more, that in the mouth of two or three witnesses every word may be established. And if he shall neglect to hear them, tell it unto the Church; but if he neglect to hear the Church, let him be unto thee as an heathen man and a publican."

When the two forms of private remonstrance have failed, the case is to be brought before the society at large. The appeal is to be made not to the rulers of the congregation, but to the congregation itself and the public opinion of the Church is to be brought to bear upon the offender. Should he defy that opinion and persist in his evil-doing, he practically excommunicates himself. All societies are justified in excluding from their communion one who repudiates the very conditions of membership : and his being regarded as 'a heathen and a publican' is but the legitimate consequence of his own act. Although they thus became as outcasts and no longer could be treated as brothers, yet they were still human beings and were to be the subjects of pity and Christian forbearance.

The promise before made to Peter is now extended not only to the other Apostles, but to the whole society of which they were the representatives. So far as the

[1] S. Matt. xviii. 15—17.

Church was true to its Lord and guided by His Spirit, it was not to think its decisions depended on any temporal power. They were clothed, as truth and righteousness are ever clothed, with a divine authority. Our Lord gives here the promise that whatever his immediate disciples did, acting on the commission received from Him, should be ratified in heaven.

Thus special powers, whatever they may have been, were entrusted to Christ's Apostles and early disciples for the building up of His Church upon earth, in the same way as they had some power of performing miracles.

We learn from Origen who wrote about A.D. 203— 254 that the Bishops then claimed their powers from this same promise, for he says[1] "the Bishops having received the keys of the kingdom of Heaven from Christ, teach that those who have been bound by them are bound in heaven, and those who have been loosed, that is, have received remission, are loosed in heaven." But there is no evidence that this power was assumed further than the discipline of the Church required.

To this Dr H. C. Lea adds[2] "thus in some Churches the bishops were claiming the power of the keys, but in others, their pretensions were ridiculed. Origen tells us that they cited the text in Matthew as though they held the power to bind and to loose; this is well if they can perform the works for which Christ made

---

[1] Origen, bk. III. Hom. I, in Matt.: Quoniam autem qui Episcopatus vendicant locum utuntur hoc textu, quemadmodum Petrus, et claves regni cœlorum acceptas habentes a Christo, docent quoniam qui ab eis ligati fuerint, in cœlo esse ligatos, et qui ab eis soluti fuerint, id est remissionem acceperint, esse in cœlo solutos.

[2] H. C. Lea, Auricular Confession, Vol. I. p. 111.

the grant to Peter, but it is absurd in him, who is bound in the chains of his own sins, to pretend to loosen others, simply because he is called a bishop."

Whatever this power of binding and loosing, of remitting or retaining, may have been understood to be in the various ages of the Church, whether it was in reference to the expulsion and reconciliation of offending members of the Christian community, or what was assumed by the leading Bishops and rulers of the Church, as a sacerdotal authority over the souls of men—this is outside the subject which I have in hand and which I will as much as possible avoid, though connected with it so closely that many were in the dark ages of the Church led to make Confession of their sins under the idea that they could by this power of the Priests be exonerated from any further penalty of their wickedness.

Public Confession of unbelief and worldly sinfulness.

There is then the passage in S. Matthew's Gospel[1], "Then went out to him Jerusalem and all Judæa and all the region round about Jordan, and were baptized of him, confessing their sins." The word used in the Greek (ἐξομολογούμενοι, translated "confessing") implies public utterance, and included a specific mention of the more grievous individual sins. The term ἐξομολόγησις[2] by

---

[1] S. Matt. iii. 5, 6.

[2] Tertullian de Pænitentia, cap. 9: Is actus, qui magis Græco vocabulo exprimitur et frequentatur, exomologesis est, qua delictum Domino nostro confitemur, non quidem ut ignaro sed quatenus satisfactio confessione disponitur confessione pænitentia nascitur, pænitentia Deus mitigatur......Itaque exomologesis prosternendi et humilificandi hominis disciplina est.

which confession is designated in the New Testament came in time to signify the whole act of confession to God with prostration and humiliation, whereby repentance was excited, and through which His wrath might be appeased.

This meaning is also the same as employed by S. Cyprian in the third century in his Tract de Lapsis, when speaking of those who had been guilty of *apostasy* and had offered meat to idols, venturing to partake of the Holy Eucharist[1] "before they have in any manner endeavoured to satisfy for their offence, before they have made a *solemn confession* of it, before any notification of their pardon, by imposition of the bishop's hands, and admission to the Holy Eucharist, before it is by any of these marks apparent that the anger of God against them is appeased : they are so weak as to imagine that peace is restored to them, because some few as weak as themselves, and as unqualified to give it, are forward enough to promise it."

What then do we learn from this passage of S. Matthew? Let us try to picture to our minds the scene there described. Crowds, who had had their consciences awakened by the preaching of John the Baptist, pressed around him and as they presented themselves for immersion in the river, confessed in turn their sins and through this baptism they became enrolled as his followers. They by repentance had determined upon a thorough change of life and character, and to avoid in future those evil

---

[1] Cyprian de Lapsis, ch. xiv.: Ante expiata delicta, ante *exomologesin* factam criminis, ante purgatam conscientiam sacrificio et manu sacerdotis, ante offensam placatam indignantis Domini et minantis, pacem putant esse, quam quidam verbis fallacibus venditant.

courses, in which they had before so freely indulged. From the circumstances of the case the terms of their confession must have been short indeed, and probably would take some such form as the following : " I have committed murder or adultery or theft " or " I have been living by plunder or dishonesty or in unbelief of God "; " I will try to live differently in future ": or it may have taken the simple and less precise form of the Publican's prayer " God, be merciful to me, a sinner." This Confession was of a most public character and on the face of it has reference to their religious faith : they acknowledge their past sinful lives and imply their previous unbelief in Christ Jesus of Nazareth as the Messiah.   They are impressed by the preaching of John the Baptist with the conviction that they have been living a life of sin, following after their own will and passions, plunging into sinful pleasures of vice and immorality, neglecting to search out the will of God as to the way they should walk—the words of the Baptist strike home to their hearts, they see the error of their ways and they confess that they have been living without a thought of God, and they determine to seek repentance and the guidance of one, who is appointed to prepare the way of the Lord.

Let us now consider a passage in the Acts of the Apostles[1]. "And many that believed came and confessed and shewed their deeds. Many of them also which used curious arts, brought their books together and burned them before all men : and they counted the price of them and found it 50,000 pieces of silver. So mightily grew the word of God and prevailed."

[1] Acts xix. 18—20.

There can be but little doubt from the manner in which this is narrated that the confession was made publicly before the people then assembled together: [1] "Fear fell on them all and the name of the Lord Jesus was magnified," for it was soon known throughout the city of Ephesus that the evil spirit had overcome the seven sons of Sceva, the Jew, who, though unbelievers, had dared to call over him the name of Jesus. Some felt staggered at the effect of a power which they could not trace, others connected this display of maddened rage with One who had seemingly resented the improper use of His name: the conscience of these witnesses was awakened, the sins of their past lives came suddenly back to their memories and they found relief in confessing and unburdening their souls of their former wickedness.

Some confessed that they had been plying a wicked trade with the credulous and ignorant populace, and in proof that they were resolved to give it up, they burnt their books of divination and made a return to their former calling impossible.

This then was a public confession of their former trust in augury, charms and magical arts, being an error of great magnitude, and they desire to enter upon a new and better life, and to accept the faith in Christ, the Son of the living and true God, concerning whom Paul preached, and to live henceforth as Christian men ought to live.

[1] Acts xix. 17.

Mutual Confession of sins among Christian brethren.

This appears to be the drift of the passage in the Epistle of S. James[1] : "Is any sick among you? let him call for the elders of the Church: and let them pray over him, anointing him with oil in the name of the Lord; and the prayer of faith shall save the sick, and the Lord shall raise him up: and if he have committed sins, they shall be forgiven him. Confess your faults one to another, that ye may be healed. The effectual fervent prayer of a righteous man availeth much."

Bishop Harold Browne observes on this passage[2] : "Here unction was evidently an outward sign, similar to that used by our Saviour, when He made clay, and put it to the blind man's eyes. It was connected with the miraculous power of healing." The sick man appears to be suffering the consequence of some sin that he has committed, for, says Bede, "many by reason of sins done in the soul are compassed by weakness, nay even death of the body." The Apostle is enforcing the efficacy of the prayer of faith in afflictions, "Is any among you afflicted? let him pray." So in sickness let the sick man inform the elders of the Church. Let them, representing the congregation of the faithful, pray over the sick man, and as the Apostles, when first commissioned[3], "anointed with oil many that were sick and healed them," so the elders when summoned to the presence of the sick man, were to anoint him with oil in the name of the Lord. "And the prayer of faith

---

[1] S. James v. 14—16.

[2] Exposition of the 39 Articles by Bishop H. Browne, p. 589.

[3] S. Mark vi. 13.

shall save the sick, and the Lord shall raise him up."
The aim of the apostolic anointing was bodily recovery,
and as Bishop Browne asserts "this exactly corresponds
with the miraculous cures of early ages...so long as such
powers remained in the Church, it was reasonable that
anointing of the sick should be retained." "Confess
therefore one to another, not only to the elders, but to
one another, your transgressions, and pray for one
another, that ye may be healed of your sickness."

Hooker tells us on this passage[1] "that we cannot
certainly affirm sacramental confession to have been
meant or spoken of in this place" though it is on these
words of S. James that those writers, who uphold the
Romish doctrine of the necessity of confessing sins to a
priest, place so much confidence: but this Bellarmine
does at the expense of the literal meaning of words of
the text, for he says[2], "confess ye one to another"
is nothing else than confess ye men to men, those
who need Absolution to those who have the power
of absolving.

Now this direction of S. James "confess your faults
one to another" is probably the only passage in the
New Testament that advises us to confess our sins to
any other than God Himself. S. James is speaking to
the afflicted and to the sick: and he exhorts men under
those circumstances to seek consolation through mutual
prayer: and in order that the prayer may be mutual,
he advises them to confess to one another their faults[3].

---

[1] Hooker, E. P. bk. vi. p. 24.

[2] Bellarmine De Pæn. lib. iii. ch. iv.; "Confitemini alter utrum"
nihil est aliud nisi confitemini homines hominibus, qui Absolutione
indigetis, illis, qui potestatem habent absolvendi.

[3] Dr Hook, The Church and its Ordinances, Vol. II. p. 224.

The elders of the Church are the most likely persons, from experience and knowledge, to be able advisers when the fear of death gains possession of a sick and sinful man. From such an one the sinner hopes not for grace but for comfort and for guidance as to the better channel of his thoughts.

In the 2nd Part of the Sermon on Repentance[1] issued in 1559 we read "the adversaries go about to wrest this place, for to maintain their Auricular Confession withal, they are greatly deceived themselves and do shamefully deceive others : for if this text ought to be understood of auricular confession, then the priests are as much bound to confess themselves unto the lay-people, as the lay-people are bound to confess themselves to them. And if to pray is to absolve, then the laity by this place hath as great authority to absolve the priests, as the priests have to absolve the laity."

There can be very little doubt that in the early Church, when S. Paul was planting a Church in each of the various towns of importance, which he visited on his missionary journeys, there was every endeavour to put down vice among the enrolled members of the Christian society as well as denouncing evil among the people at large, and striving to call them into the household of faith.

The action of S. Paul and the Church towards one guilty of incest.

A member of the Corinthian Church had made himself notorious as an evil-doer and S. Paul commands

---

[1] 1559, Sermon on Repentance, S.P.C.K. p. 575.

the Church of Corinth to have no dealings with a man, who has committed the sin of incest by marrying his father's wife, and[1] "to deliver such an one to Satan for the destruction of the flesh, that the Spirit may be saved in the day of our Lord Jesus Christ." He bids them[2] "put away from among yourselves the wicked person." The man is practically to be excommunicated, and is 'bound' by the Apostle. This seems to have had the desired effect, and it seems that the man undertook to have no further intercourse with this woman and· must have acknowledged that it was wrong and against the law of God : he probably implored forgiveness and appealed to the Apostle to plead for his restoration to a share in those Christian privileges, which he had forfeited. His sorrow for having committed this wickedness must have been considered by the Apostle sincere, for within a twelvemonth S. Paul 'looses' him and asks for his restoration and forgiveness by the Corinthian Church, and states that he had forgiven the man[3] "in the face of Christ."

From this we see that in the time of S. Paul, the Church exercised a power of excommunicating notorious sinners and when they were brought to acknowledge the evil of their ways and to be sincere in their repentance the Bishop and Pastors of the flock restored the penitent to his place among them. This was a discipline not only between the sinner and an offended God, but between the sinner and a scandalised Church.

[1] 1 Cor. v. 5.   [2] 1 Cor. v. 13.
[3] 2 Cor. ii. 10.

CHAPTER II.

BEFORE considering further the question of Confession as practised in Christ's Church after the time of 'the records of this matter given us in the New Testament, it is well to state that though all sin deprives us of the favour of Almighty God, we can only obtain reconciliation with Him by making Confession to Him and by praying for forgiveness, relying on the merits of Christ's death and feeling the inward secret Repentance of the heart, being moved with true sorrow for the sin committed and determining by God's help to avoid such sin for the future. Nevertheless man must not forget that though all sin is an offence against God, yet it may also be a cause of injury to his fellow-man or a scandal to the society to which he belongs. If he has sinned so as to do a wrong to his neighbour—he cannot be true in his repentance unless he make all the amends in his power for the injury he has effected on another. And so too if he commits a sin in violation of his express undertaking when he was enrolled a member of Christ's Church that he would fight under the banner of Christ as His faithful soldier and servant against the world, the flesh, and the Devil—he walks out of the fold of the Church and must seek a restoration to its privileges

and Communion, if he desires them, by an acknow- A.D. 54
ledgment of his wrong-doing and by an amendment of
life.

S. Barnabas, or an Epistle which bears his name,
says, "Thou shalt confess thy sins, and not come to
thy Prayer with an evil conscience[1];" as prayer is to be
offered to God alone, it is plain that the confession is
to be made to Him.

Enrolment of members of the Christian Church without any term of probation.

Now on the great day of Pentecost when S. Peter
addressed a large assembly of Jews, devout men out of
every nation under heaven, we read in the Acts of the
Apostles[2] that 3000 gladly received his word and were
baptized, and were enrolled as members of Christ's
Church. Here there was evidently no lengthened period
of preparation and mourning for their previous disbelief
in Christ as the Messiah, though probably there was a
confession to the extent that they now believed.

Spread of Christianity among Gentile nations.

These persons, that were moved by the words of
S. Peter, in his memorable sermon, would return to
their homes and spread the knowledge of the Gospel
in the distant lands of the then known world. We have
the tracing of the Apostolic journeys of S. Paul, with

---

[1] Catholic Ep. of S. Barnabas, § 19: Ἐξομολογήσῃ ἐπὶ ἁμαρτίαις
σου. Οὐχ ἥξεις ἐν προσευχῇ (ἐπὶ προσευχήν) σου ἐν συνειδήσει πονηρᾷ.
Dr Wake's Trans. A.D. 1719, p. 193.

[2] Acts ii. 41.

R. 2

details of the treatment he received in many cities and of the success of his labours. We are told that when at Corinth[1] "he testified to the Jews that Jesus was Christ," and when they opposed themselves and blasphemed, he shook his raiment and said unto them, "Your blood be upon your own heads; I am clean: from henceforth I will go unto the Gentiles." We know also how in the case of Cornelius at Cæsarea, S. Peter and afterwards the Apostles and brethren in Judæa were convinced that "God hath also to the Gentiles granted repentance unto life[2]." And tradition tells us, S. James alone remaining in charge of the Church at Jerusalem, that most of the Apostles made their way into distant countries and established the Church of Christ everywhere.

Thus the converts consisted not only of the educated Jew and Gentile in civilised places but also of ignorant people even among heathen races, whose life and passions were guided by no laws, civil or religious. Such persons had hitherto been living only under such laws as nature and their own inclination taught them, and it could scarcely be expected that immediately after their consciences had been awakened by Christian teachers, they would alter their whole character according to the strict morality required of the followers of Christ. These converts in the early days of Christianity were at first enrolled at once or after only a probation of two or three days, when it was hoped that their heart would be moved to restrain the evil of their nature when they had placed themselves under the guidance of spiritual teachers.

[1] Acts xviii. 5, 6.   [2] Acts xi. 18.

A term of probation for catechumens was appointed.

Towards the end of the 2nd century the term of probation was considerably increased, and none were admitted to the rite of baptism until they had for a period of three months mourned over their delinquencies and sought pardon of God by prayer, assisted by the supplications of the congregation of the faithful, and they were then after promises of amendment of life and of departure from the sins of their earlier days, admitted to the solemn rite of Baptism, whereby they received the assurance of divine help and of God's pardon.

Now if we consult the 1st Epistle of S. Clement to the Corinthians, which was written about A.D. 95, we A.D. 95 learn what manner of confession was recommended in those early days. He writes[1], "Being full of good designs, ye did with great readiness of mind and with a religious confidence, stretch forth your hand to God Almighty, beseeching Him to be merciful unto you, if in anything ye had unwillingly sinned against Him." And again in the same Epistle, he writes[2], "Beloved, God is not indigent of anything : nor does He demand anything of us, but that we should confess our sins unto Him. For so says the Holy David[3], 'I will confess unto the Lord and it shall please Him better than a

---

[1] S. Clement, 1 Ep. to Cor. § 2: μεστοί τε ὁσίας βουλῆς ἐν ἀγαθῇ προθυμίᾳ μετ᾽ εὐσεβοῦς πεποιθήσεως ἐξετείνατε τὰς χεῖρας ὑμῶν πρὸς τὸν παντοκράτορα Θεόν, ἱκετεύοντες αὐτὸν ἵλεως γενέσθαι εἴ τι ἄκοντες ἡμάρτετε.

[2] S. Clement, 1 Ep. to Cor. § 52: Οὐδὲν οὐδενὸς χρῄζει, εἰ μὴ τὸ ἐξομολογεῖσθαι αὐτῷ.

[3] Ps. lxix. 31.

young bullock.'" And a little further on in the same
Epistle he says[1], "Do ye therefore submit yourselves unto
your Priests, and be instructed unto repentance, bending
the knees of your hearts. Learn to be subject, laying
aside all proud and arrogant wilfulness of speech, for it
is better to be found in the flock of Christ, little and
well thought of, than being reckoned overbearing, to be
cast out of His fold (or quarters)."

This last, as Marshall observes, refers to the penitential discipline, of which succeeding writers give us
further accounts. S. Clement exhorts them to submit
to discipline[2], a discipline which consisted in expelling
offenders from the fold of Christ: or rather from that
enclosure which parted the faithful from penitents and
hearers in the assemblies for worship.

In the 2nd Epistle to the Corinthians, ascribed to
S. Clement, he makes mention of 'outward confession[3]'
and 'visible acts of penance' as existing at that time—
thus, "For after we have gone out of this world we
can no longer there make our confession, or do our
penance."

Whenever the Fathers speak of the necessity of
confession they consider it, (i) as the door to a course
of public penance, which humbled the penitent, subjected

[1] S. Clement, 1 Ep. to Cor. § 57: Ὑμεῖς οὖν...ὑποταγῆτε τοῖς πρεσ-
βυτέροις, καὶ παιδευθῆτε εἰς μετάνοιαν, κάμψαντες τὰ γόνατα τῆς καρδίας
ὑμῶν, μάθετε ὑποτάσσεσθαι ἀποθέμενοι τὴν ἀλαζόνα καὶ ὑπερήφανον τῆς
γλώσσης ὑμῶν αὐθάδειαν. ἄμεινον γάρ ἐστιν ὑμῖν ἐν τῷ ποιμνίῳ τοῦ Χριστοῦ
μικροὺς καὶ ἐλλογίμους εὑρεθῆναι ἢ καθ' ὑπεροχὴν δοκοῦντας ἐκριφῆναι ἐκ
τῆς ἐλπίδος (κιγλίδος or ἐπαυλίδος) αὐτοῦ. Dr Wake's Trans. A.D.
1693.

[2] Marshall's Penitential Discipline, p. 21.

[3] Clement, 2 Ep. to Cor. § 8: Μετὰ γὰρ τὸ ἐξελθεῖν ἡμᾶς ἐκ τοῦ
κόσμου, οὐκέτι δυνάμεθα ἐκεῖ, ἐξομολογήσασθαι ἢ μετανοεῖν ἔτι.

him to a healthful discipline (which privately, it were to be feared, few would practise) and kept him for awhile from the Holy Communion, which might be hurtful to him, (ii) as obtaining for individuals spiritual counsel for the specific case of each, (iii) as gaining the intercessions of the Church, and so of Christ[1]. The Apostles and those that had heard them, and seen their miracles, bid men turn from their heedless and sinful mode of life, and raise themselves from sin to a life of righteousness and become followers of Christ, who had redeemed them by the sacrifice of Himself on the Cross. Men were called to a higher and holier life, no longer to live unto themselves, but unto God.

The spread of Christianity was marvellous.

Churches or bodies of Christians were thus established in many parts of the world at a distance from Jerusalem. Soon after the day of Pentecost, the knowledge of the faith was spread through most of the countries which border on the Mediterranean Sea. A clear account of S. Paul's journeys and labours is given us in the Acts of the Apostles. S. Peter[2] is said to have founded the Church at Antioch, and, after regulating its affairs for seven years, to have visited Parthia and other countries of the East: and finally settled at

---

[1] Tertullian, Note M, p. 380.

[2] Hieron. de V. Illust. § 1: Simon Petrus, post episcopatum Antiochensis Ecclesiæ, Romam pergit, ibique viginti quinque annis Cathedram Sacerdotalem tenuit. Andreas frater hujus, ut majores nostri prodiderunt, Scythis, et Sogdianis, et Saccis prædicavit Evangelium Domini nostri Jesu Christi, et in Sebastopoli prædicavit.

Rome, where he became Bishop. S. Bartholomew[1] is said to have preached in India and Arabia, S. Andrew[2] in Scythia, S. Matthew and S. Matthias in Ethiopia. The Church of Alexandria traced itself to S. Mark, and the Christianity of Africa was most probably derived from Rome by means of teachers whose memory has perished.

The three great sins, which were specially to be avoided.

A.D. 52   We are told in the Acts of the Apostles[3] that at Antioch there was great dissension touching circumcision, and that the matter was referred to the Apostles and elders at Jerusalem. They called together a Council, at which S. James presided. After there had been much disputing Peter, Barnabas and Paul addressed the assembly, and finally James gave sentence that " we trouble not them which from among the Gentiles are turned to God : but that we write unto them, that they abstain from pollution of idols, and from fornication, and from things strangled, and from blood." Now Jerusalem, the city where the Church had taken its beginning, had naturally been regarded by Christians as a religious centre. But the destruction of the Temple and the Holy City by Titus in the year A.D. 70 put an end to this position, and

---

[1] Eusebius, v. 10: Οἷς (᾽Ινδοῖς) Βαρθολομαῖον τῶν ἀποστόλων ἕνα κηρύξαι.

[2] Eusebius iii. 1 : Τὰ μὲν δὴ κατὰ ᾽Ιουδαίους ἐν τούτοις ἦν. Τῶν δὲ ἱερῶν τοῦ Σωτῆρος ἡμῶν ἀποστόλων τε καὶ μαθητῶν ἐφ᾽ ἅπασαν κατασπαρέντων τὴν οἰκουμένην. Θωμᾶς μὲν, ὡς ἡ παράδοσις περιέχει, τὴν Παρθίαν εἴληχεν, ᾽Ανδρέας δὲ τὴν Σκυθίαν, ᾽Ιωάννης τὴν ᾽Ασίαν, πρὸς οἷς καὶ διατρίψας ἐν ᾽Εφέσῳ τελευτᾷ.

[3] Acts xv.

the Church of Jerusalem no longer stood in its former relation of superiority to other Churches. The converts were many and of every nation, of various degrees of intellectual power and of moral fitness. They were especially surrounded by temptations not to continue steadfast in the new faith they had adopted. Thus there soon arose the necessity of some rules of discipline for recognized membership of the Church of Christ. After the destruction of the Church at Jerusalem every district branch of the Church had to determine its own conditions of fellowship, and when a member was found guilty of such gross sins as S. James in his judgment bid them abstain from, he was not allowed to be a partaker of the Holy Communion until his repentance and amendment satisfied the rulers of his congregation. Considering who the converts were and that many had been brought up to worship idols, and to whom it was no shame to indulge in vicious habits, to consider self the first law of nature, to pamper their evil passions in every conceivable way, it is no wonder that some broke through the strict moral laws of Christianity and came under the censure of the rulers of the Church, into which they had been admitted. The laxity of their former life and the influence of those members of their family and acquaintance who had not embraced the Christian religion were likely in some measure to lead them astray. Besides this, those who were suspected of having become converts were frequently threatened with torture or with death by the rulers of their nation unless they would sacrifice to idols as heretofore. These defaulters, who had committed the gross sins of idolatry (including heresy), unchastity or homicide, were shut out from the Church, debarred from receiving the Holy Communion, and so continued until they had given evidence of remorse by confessing the sin committed and enduring such penalties as the chief rulers of the Church deemed necessary. Such persons were often described as being ' excommunicated.'

Open Confession for notorious or gross sins.

Anyone that had assumed membership in the Church of Christ, having been admitted thereto through the door of Baptism, would naturally feel uneasy in conscience when he had committed one of the gross sins, which, when known, shut him out from the high privilege of partaking of the Holy Communion. When such a shameful sin came to the ears of the congregation and its chief Pastor the offender was by the latter closely questioned upon the matter, and if he admitted that he was guilty, he was required to make full confession of his guilt before the assembled congregation and then to go through a course of humiliation and penance, seeking the prayers of the priest and people to intercede with God for his pardon—when he had completed his course and showed sufficient signs of true repentance for his sins, he was re-admitted by the ceremony of the laying on of hands by the Bishop and restored to full membership and Communion. Persons who were guilty of such great offences were encouraged to make complete confession of their own accord, without any accusation being brought against them, by the promise that their penance would be of shorter duration, as such a voluntary confession would be deemed a good sign of sorrow for their sin. Thus it became a rule of discipline, mostly enforced throughout the sphere of the various Churches, that sinners, who had committed one of the three gross sins of idolatry, immorality or homicide, either voluntarily or after accusation and condemnation openly confessed such sin before the congregation to which they belonged.

Towards the close of the 1st century, S. Clement of Rome[1] assumes that repentance and prayer to God for pardon suffice, but strongly recommends intercessory prayer for those who have fallen into sin.

About the same period S. Barnabas advocates almsgiving as a means of redeeming sins, writing thus— "Thou shalt also labour with thy hands, 'to give to the poor,' that thy sins may be forgiven thee[2]."

Such persons as stood convicted of notorious sin were subjected to public penance[3].

But for lesser sins[4], repentant sinners endeavoured to make their peace with God by mortification and almsgiving, and occasionally by confession of their sins: they often sought the advice of priest or bishop, as those best able to direct them, and they asked the prayers of the congregation to intercede for them with God.

The Shepherd of Hermas[5] seems to know only of

---

[1] Clement, Ep. i ad Cor. viii. 1 ; xxii. 1 ; xxiii. 1, 15.

[2] S. Barnabas, Ep. § 19: καὶ διὰ τῶν χειρῶν σου ἐργάσῃ εἰς λύτρωσιν τῶν ἁμαρτιῶν σου. Trans. by Dr Wake, edition 1719.

[3] Dr Pusey, Gaume, p. xlv.

[4] Dr Lea, vol. I. p. 18.

[5] Sancti Hermæ Pastor Lib. II. Mand. i: Primum omnium credere quod unus est Deus...et time eum et timens, habe abstinentiam. Hæc custodi, et abjice abs te omnem nequitiam, et indue virtutem justitiæ et vives Deo si custodieris mandatum hoc.

Ib. Lib. I. Visio III. § ix: Ego vos enutrivi in multa simplicitate et innocentia et modestia propter misericordiam Dei, quæ super vos

confession to God, which with repentance, prayer and
faith procures pardon : though he enjoins penance for sins.

After the fall of Jerusalem and the consequent
scattering of the Christians of the Church of that City,
there was no central or chief Church to which to refer
differences of faith or discipline and so a uniformity of
practice was no longer maintained. The discipline of
each Church, as stated above, was regulated and enforced
by the Bishop of the district, who sometimes in cases of
difficulty or doubt consulted with his Episcopal brethren
within his reach.

Eusebius informs us that "Dionysius[1] of Corinth (in
the 2nd century), the Areopagite, having been converted
to the faith by the Apostle Paul, writes to the Church
which is at Amastris and bids them receive back those
who have returned with amendment of life from any
falling away, whether of mistake or heretical error," but
he does not prescribe any formalities to be observed or
gone through.

stillavit in justitia: ut sanctificemini et justificemini ab omni nequitia
et omni pravitate.

Hermæ Pastor, Lib. II. Mand. iii.: Qui ergo mentiuntur, abnegant
Dominum, non reddentes Deo depositum quod acceperunt.

Ib., Lib. III. Simil. vii.: Oportet eum qui agit pœnitentiam affligere
animam suam et humilem animose præstare in omni negotio et vexa-
tiones multas variasque perferre; cumque perpessus fuerit omnia quæ
illi instituta fuerint, tunc forsitan qui eum creavit et qui formavit universa, commovebitur erga eum clementia sua et aliquod remedium dabit;
idque ita, si viderit ejus, qui pœnitentiam agit, cor purum esse ab omni
opere nequissimo.

[1] Eusebius, H. E. bk. IV. § 23: Διονύσιος ὁ Ἀρεοπαγίτης ὑπὸ τοῦ
Ἀποστόλου Παύλου προτραπεὶς ἐπὶ τὴν πίστιν...τοὺς ἐξ οἵας δ' οὖν ἀποπτώ-
σεως, εἴτε πλημμελείας, εἴτε μὴν αἱρετικῆς πλάνης ἐπιστρέφοντας, δεξιοῦσθαι
προστάττει.

How a case of adultery was dealt with.

We have the testimony of Irenæus, Bishop of Lyons A.D. 178 A.D. 178, as to the course imposed by the Church in a sad case of "adultery." He relates[1] that the wife of a deacon had been corrupted by Marcus, and states that she was brought to feel her guilt after much labour on the part of the brethren, and that then she passed the rest of her life in penitential humiliations, and in that solemn "exhomologesis" which was a part of penance in such cases; the words "on the part of the brethren" would naturally signify that her confession had been made before the Church rather than to a single priest. And so also in the case of other women, which Irenæus tells us had been corrupted by the same heretic Marcus.

How a case of heresy was dealt with.

Irenæus also mentions the undergoing of public penance by one guilty of "heretical teaching[2]." A certain man named Cerdon, coming into the Church and performing penance (ἐξομολογούμενος), he thus continued [to the end,] at one time teaching privily, at another performing penance, at another convicted by some as to the things

---

[1] Irenæus, Lib. I. ch. 13: Τῆς γυναικὸς αὐτοῦ εὐειδοῦς ὑπαρχούσης καὶ τὴν γνώμην, καὶ τὸ σῶμα διαφθαρείσης ὑπὸ τοῦ μάγου τούτου, καὶ ἐξακολουθησάσης αὐτῷ πολλῷ τῷ χρόνῳ· ἔπειτα μετὰ πολλοῦ κόπου τῶν ἀδελφῶν ἐπιστρεψάντων, αὐτὴ τὸν ἅπαντα χρόνον ἐξομολογουμένη διετέλεσε πειθοῦσα καὶ θρηνοῦσα ἐφ᾽ ᾗ ἔπαθεν ὑπὸ τοῦ μάγου διαφθορᾷ.

[2] Irenæus, Lib. III. ch. 4: Κέρδων δὲ ὁ πρὸ Μαρκίωνος, καὶ αὐτὸς ἐπὶ Ὑγίνου, ὃς ἦν ἔνατος ἐπίσκοπος εἰς τὴν Ἐκκλησίαν ἐλθὼν, καὶ ἐξομολογούμενος οὕτως διετέλεσε, ποτὲ μὲν λαθροδιδασκαλῶν, ποτὲ δὲ πάλιν ἐξομολογούμενος ποτὲ δὲ ἐλεγχόμενος ἐφ᾽ οἷς ἐδίδασκε κακῶς, καὶ ἀφιστάμενος τῆς τῶν ἀδελφῶν συνοδίας.

which he taught perversely, and put out of the society of the brethren.

Bellarmine[1] draws the conclusion from these two passages that Irenæus used the word "exhomologesis" to signify the confession of secret, or hidden crimes, and that this confession was made to the priest, who appointed what "satisfaction was necessary," whereas the continuance of the "exhomologesis" would imply a period of humiliation in the Church after confession of the sin, even though a secret one, had been publicly made before the brethren.

So that persons performing penance may fairly be presumed to have made a confession of their sins or at least of that sin for which they undergo penance. Sometimes under the direction of a priest, who had been privately consulted, or being moved by a sudden contrition and remorse some would charge themselves with a secret sin before the congregation. In this way "*public confession of secret sins*" was occasionally practised by sensitive offenders. It is evident by the above descriptions given by Irenæus that though he describes the confessions by the term "homologesis" he means a whole course of penance, which was then imposed on such sinners, and consisted of outward gestures, as of weeping, groaning and accusing themselves. Penitents were re-

---

[1] Bellarmine de Pœn. Lib. III. ch. 6: Exhomologesis loquitur de occulto crimine, immo etiam de occulta cupiditate, quæ nisi ex confessione fœminarum illarum cognosci non potuisset, in lib. autem 3. c. 4 apertissime Irenæus dicit, Cerdonem Exhomologesim fecisse, postquam latenter hæresim suam docuerat: Quare loquitur in utroque loco de confessione secretorum sive occultorum scelerum....

Sacerdos audita Confessione, disponit atque ordinat, quæ satisfactio necessaria sit, et ea pœnitenti injungit.

quired to practise every kind of self-denial and humili- ation, they were excluded from the body of the church, were regarded as outcasts and denied all privileges of the services of the Church and of participating in the blessings of the Holy Communion, and when they had finished the penance imposed on them[1], they were led from the porch to the middle of the church, when the Bishop placed them before the Presbyters, Deacons, widows and people, where they again lay on the ground, bewailed their offences, wept largely, commending themselves to the prayers of all, solemnly vowing never to relapse into the same. The Bishop after this restored them by "the laying on of hands" to full membership of the Church and they were again allowed to be partakers of the Holy Communion. But this confession of *secret* sins was still *voluntary*. Clement of Alexandria[2] about A.D. 200 seems to imply that some ministers judged who were or who were not worthy to be partakers of the Holy Communion, though he himself thought the individual conscience the best guide. So that in his day confession was not held as necessary before approaching the Lord's Table.

Tertullian's views as to penance[3], which involved confession to the priest or people, are of the severest

[1] *Albaspinæus, note f. on Note L. on Tertullian, p. 377, Oxf. 1842.

[2] Clement of Alexandria, Strom. or Miscellanies I. 1: ἢ καὶ τὴν Εὐχαριστίαν τινὲς διανείμαντες ὡς ἔθος αὐτὸν δὴ ἕκαστον τοῦ λαοῦ λαβεῖν τὴν μοῖραν ἐπιτρέπουσιν, ἀρίστη γὰρ πρὸς τὴν ἀκριβῆ αἵρεσίν τε καὶ φυγὴν, ἡ συνείδησις.

[3] Tertullian, Apolog. adv. Gent. c. 39: Ibidem etiam exhortationes, castigationes et censura Divina. Nam et judicatur magno cum pondere, ut apud certos de Dei conspectu; summumque futuri judicii præjudicium est, si quis ita deliquerit, ut a communicatione orationis et conventus et omnis sancti commercii relegetur.

kind, and he very clearly states that those who are guilty
of heinous sin are excluded from the communion of the
Church. There are, says he, exhortations, rebukes, and
the great holy censure; for sentence there is passed with
the utmost gravity and consideration, as among a people
who are always sensible that they are in the presence of
God: and it is esteemed a notable presumption that the
judgment of God will confirm the sentence thus passed
by man when any one so offends amongst us, as to be
cut off from all communion both in prayer and in
assembling ourselves together, and in all holy offices
whatsoever.

Now what we learn from Origen refers to Confession
as a part of the penance then prescribed. "If we have
sinned in any of these things, let him declare the sin
which he hath sinned[1]." And "If we anticipate him in
life and are ourselves our own accusers, we escape the
malice of the Devil, our enemy and accuser, for so the
Prophet elsewhere says, 'Tell thou thine iniquities before
(thou be accused), that thou mayest be justified,' and
David also in the same spirit saith in the Psalms, 'I
made bare mine iniquity and hid not my sins.'" From

---

[1] Origen, Hom. III. in Lev. v. 3: Si peccaverit unum aliquid de
istis, pronunciet peccatum, quod peccavit.... Si quid in occulto geri-
mus, si quid in sermone solo vel etiam intra cogitationum secreta commisimus cuncta necesse est publicari, cuncta proferri. Proferri autem
ab illo, qui et accusator peccati est, et incentor. Ipse enim nunc nos ut
peccemus, instigat, ipse etiam cum peccaverimus, accusat. Si ergo in
hac vita præveniamus eum, et ipsi nostri accusatores simus, nequitiam
diaboli inimici nostri, et accusatoris effugimus. Sic enim et alibi
propheta dicit, "Dic tu (inquit) iniquitates tuas prior, ut justificeris."
Nonne evidenter mysterium, de quo tractamus ostendit, cum dicit 'Dic
tu prior.' Sed et David eodem spiritu loquitur, in psalmis et dicit,
"Iniquitatem meam notam feci, et peccatum meum non cooperui."

these passages we see that, (i) the confession relates not A.D. 230 to that made to man but to God, as appears from the Scriptures quoted, (ii) as far as it does involve acknowledgement of sin before man, it relates to public penance when he states that there is a 7th remission of sin through penitence, when the sinner "washeth his bed with his tears" and "his tears become his bread day and night, and when he shrinks not from shewing to the priests of the Lord his sin."

Origen in his Homily II. on Psalm xxxvii. gives us very precise directions when a sinner is overburdened with the weight of his sin that he should open his grief to a discreet priest, who he thinks would be likely to sympathize with him in his distress and to give him the best directions for obtaining relief.

Private Confession with a view to public penance.

Origen advocates voluntary confession, and thus advises[1]: "As they who are troubled with indigestion

---

[1] Origen, Hom. II. on Ps. xxxvii. quoted by Bingham, bk. VIII. ch. iii. § 4. Note M. on Tertullian, p. 381; Marshall, Pen. Disc. p. 35; and by Dr Pusey, 'Gaume,' p. xlvi.: Sicut ii, qui habent intus inclusam escam indigestam aut humoris vel phlegmatis stomacho graviter et moleste imminentia, si vomuerint, relevantur: ita etiam hi, qui peccaverunt, si quidem occultant et retinent intra se peccatum, intrinsecus urgentur, et prope modum suffocantur a phlegmate vel humore peccati. Si autem ipse sui accusator fiat, dum accusat semetipsum et confitetur simul evomit et delictum atque omnem morbi digerit causam. Tantummodo circumspice diligentius, cui debeas confiteri peccatum tuum. Proba prius medicum, cui debeas causam languoris exponere, qui sciat infirmari cum infirmante, flere cum flente, qui condolendi et compatiendi noverit disciplinam: ut ita demum si quid ille dixerit, qui se prius et eruditum medicum ostenderit et misericordem, si quid consilii dederit, facias et sequaris; si intellexerit et præviderit talem esse languorem

and have anything within them, which lies crude upon their stomachs, are not relieved but by proper evacuations; so sinners, who conceal their practices and retain them within their own bosoms feel in themselves an inward disquietude and are almost choked with the malignity which they thus suppress. But by confession and self-accusation, they discharge themselves of their burden and digest, as it were, the crudity which was so oppressive. Only here it will be fit to advise them, that they be careful in choosing a fit person, to whom they may open their minds with profit and advantage, that they try to find out such a spiritual physician as knows how to mourn with them that mourn, to be weak with them that are weak, in fine, to be tender and compassionate, and such an one upon the whole, as having approved his skill to them, may give them reason to depend upon his counsel and to follow it; that so, if he shall judge their case to be what may need the cure of a public animadversion and deserve to be laid open in the face of the Church, for the edification either of themselves or others, this may be done deliberately and discreetly and agreeably to the directions of such an approved physician."

From this it is clear that the confession contemplated was absolutely voluntary, and that the sinner was free to choose whom he would as one to whom he should confide his guilt and consult as to the best means to lighten his burden.

It seems more than probable that a "penitentiary" had not yet been appointed in the various dioceses,

tuum, qui in conventu totius Ecclesiæ exponi debeat et curari, ex quo fortassis et ceteri ædificari poterunt, et tu ipse facile sanari, multa hoc deliberatione et satis perito medici illius consilio procurandum est.

because when one was appointed, the choice of a confessor was clearly done away with. Origen also incidentally states that the confessor whom a penitent consulted would determine whether the matter should be made public before the whole Church (in conventu totius Ecclesiæ).

Origen has a passage, speaking directly of confession to the ministers of the Church for spiritual guidance; after having spoken of evil thoughts which should be revealed in order that they might be destroyed by Him, who died for us, he continues[1] "If we do this and confess our sins not only to God but to those also who can heal our wounds and sins, our sins will be blotted out by Him, who says 'Behold I will destroy thy iniquities as a cloud, and as a thick cloud thy sins.'"

The same Father speaks of voluntary confession before the Church[2]: "Let my kindred, if they please, forsake me and stand afar off, whilst I obtain of myself to be my own accuser and to confess my faults, when no one else would accuse me for them: whilst I do not imitate those who, when arraigned and even convicted by clear evidence, would fain, notwithstanding, conceal their crimes."

[1] Origen, Hom. XVII. in Luc.: Si enim hoc fecerimus et revelaverimus peccata nostra non solum deo, sed et his qui possunt mederi vulneribus nostris atque peccatis, delebuntur peccata nostra ab eo, qui ait 'Ecce delebo ut nubem iniquitates tuas, et sicut caliginem peccata tua.'

[2] Origen, Hom. II. Ps. xxxvii.: Licet amici mei et proximi mei contrarii sint, et propinqui mei longe se faciant a me, dum ego ipse mei accusator efficior, dum crimina mea nullo me arguente confiteor, dum nolo imitari eos qui etiam cum in judiciis arguantur, et testibus convincantur, et tortoribus etiam arguantur, tegunt tamen mala sua.

Up to the early portion of the 3rd century, hearing the confessions of penitents formed no recognized part of sacerdotal functions: this may be fairly concluded from the fact that no directions are given to priests in the Canons of Hippolytus[1] as to the course they are to adopt when penitents apply to them to receive their confessions, though these Canons minutely describe the duties of all orders of the clergy, and in them mention is only made of confession when the catechumen makes his confession to the bishop before baptism.

The public humiliation of scandalous offenders[2] was doubtless observed to carry with it very great advantages: and this might induce considerable numbers to rank themselves in the class of *public* penitents, even for their *secret* sins. Now, as in the case of *public penance for public sins*, there was a solemn humble confession of the faults for which such penance was imposed, in the face of the congregation, that what had been publicly committed in the face of the world might be publicly retracted, and thereby the scandal be removed, so in the case of *secret sins*, it is not improbable that occasion might hence be taken of thus acknowledging them in public. When this was done indiscriminately, it is easy to conceive what inconveniences might arise from it. *A penitentiary was therefore appointed* to whom these persons should resort and consult with him beforehand, what on the one hand might be fit for publication, and what on the other would be better reserved in silence. And this for a good while

---

[1] Canon. Hippolyti XIX. 103.

[2] Wheatley's Illustration of the Book of Common Prayer (Bohn), Order for the Visitation of the Sick, pp. 435, 436; Marshall's Penitential Discipline, p. 38.

was found a cure for all inconveniences until Nectarius did away with the office.

Socrates tells us that this penitentiary was appointed after the Decian persecution about A.D. 250, and the office was abolished about A.D. 500.

Public penance drifts into private penance.

Public penance was not then during this period assigned to every sin which had been privately confessed, and in process of time private penance was imposed for sins which it was deemed advisable not to confess publicly—thus penance of a public nature gradually declined and so by degrees was displaced by *private penance*.

Eusebius informs us in his valuable Church History that during the episcopate of Cornelius[1] A.D. 251 "1500 widows and destitute people received alms from the Church." The Roman Church must therefore at that time have consisted of many thousands and there were only one bishop and 46 presbyters to minister to them all, and when we consider the frequency with which the faithful communicated in the middle of the 3rd century, it would have been next to impossible that each one should make an individual confession before communicating.

It may easily be conceived that from the earliest age of the Church when a person's conscience was oppressed with grievous sin, it would be a great relief to have some

---

[1] Eusebius, H. E. VI. 43, p. 217: Ἐν ᾗ (τῇ ἐκκλησίᾳ) οὐκ ἠγνόει πρεσβυτέρους εἶναι τεσσαράκοντα ἕξ, διακόνους ἑπτά, ὑποδιακόνους ἑπτά, ἀκολούθους δύο καὶ τεσσαράκοντα ἐξορκιστὰς δὲ καὶ ἀναγνώστας ἅμα πυλωροῖς δύο καὶ πεντήκοντα, χήρας σὺν θλιβομένοις ὑπὲρ τὰς χιλίας πεντακοσίας, οὓς πάντας ἡ τοῦ Δεσπότου χάρις καὶ φιλανθρωπία διατρέφει.

A.D. 267   discreet guide and counsellor in whom the sinner could
confide and to whom he might unfold his sin with the
view of gaining advice how he might obtain relief of his
burden of sin and secure help in his prayers for mercy and
forgiveness.

In order to enforce discipline and check sin among
the members of the Church it was soon found necessary
to establish ecclesiastical courts in which the bishop sat
as judge.   Disputes and all manner of accusations as to
the character and mode of life of those who had been
enrolled as Christians were brought for hearing into such
a court, which was conducted much after the methods
of the civil courts.   Witnesses were examined and the
accused were questioned.   When the case was concluded,
the bishop passed judgment and convicted or acquitted
the accused on the evidence which had been brought
forward.   He too appointed the punishment or penance of
every one that had been proved guilty of the sin of which
he had been accused, and this penance had to be performed before he should be admitted to reconciliation.
It appears that the earliest account of such proceedings
is in the Canonical Epistle of Gregory Thaumaturgus
A.D. 267.

We learn from the Apostolical Constitutions[1] that,

---

[1] Apostol. Constit. Lib. II. c. 37, 38 Cotel.: 37. Μόνον παραλαβὼν
τὸν κατηγορηθέντα ἔλεγξον αὐτὸν ὅπως μεταγνῷ, μηδενός σοι συμπαρόντος·
εἰ δὲ οὐ πεισθείη, γενόμενος δεύτερος, ἢ τρίτος, οὕτως αὐτῷ ὑπόδειξον τὸ
πλημμέλημα, νουθετήσας αὐτὸν ἐν πρᾳότητι καὶ παιδείᾳ.

38. Ἐὰν οὖν πεισθῇ ἐπὶ στόματος τῶν τριῶν ὑμῶν, εὖ ἂν ἔχοι· εἰ δέ
τις σκληρύνοιτο, εἰπὲ τῇ ἐκκλησίᾳ· ἐὰν δὲ καὶ τῆς ἐκκλησίας παρακούσῃ,
ἔστω σοι ὡς ὁ ἐθνικὸς καὶ ὁ τελώνης· καὶ μηκέτι αὐτὸν ὡς χριστιανόν
παραδέχου ἐν τῇ ἐκκλησίᾳ, ἀλλ' ὡς ἐθνικὸν παραιτοῦ· εἰ δὲ βούλοιτο
μετανοεῖν, προσλαμβάνου.

when a crime was by any means known to have been A.D. 250
committed by a Christian, which deserved the censure of
the Church, if the party came not of his own accord
" He was convened by the bishop, first in secret, and if
he thereupon submitted and reformed, all was well;
otherwise he was to be admonished and persuaded in the
presence of two or three witnesses; and if those endeavours proved ineffectual, the whole Church was to be
acquainted with his case, and to be interested in it; and
then, if he still continued obstinately resolved against
submission, after these joint endeavours to mollify him,
the highest sentence of excommunication was finally to
be pronounced against him; under which he was to
continue, as much disregarded as a mere heathen, until
he was softened into submission and confessed and under-
went the rigours imposed upon him by the Church."

The treatment in case of 'apostasy.'

It is generally recognized as a historical fact[1] that
Decius was the first emperor who attempted to crush
out the Christian religion by a general persecution of its
professors. This persecution though severe was happily
only of short duration, from A.D. 249 to 251. The long
enjoyment of peace had told unfavourably on the Church.
Its members had grown slack in their religious observances, they wavered in their faith, and revolted against
any strictness of discipline. Cyprian[2] in the West and

[1] Robertson's Church History, Vol. I. pp. 96, 97.

[2] Cyprian, de Lapsis, 5: Ad prima statim verba minantis inimici
maximus fratrum numerus fidem suam prodidit nec prostratus est perse-
cutionis impetu, sed voluntario lapsu se ipse prostravit. Quid oro

Origen in the East speak of the secular spirit which had crept in among its members—of the pride, the luxury, the covetousness of the higher clergy, of the careless and irreligious lives of the people. And when as Origen[1] had foretold, a new season of trial came, the effects of the general relaxation were sadly displayed. On being summoned, in obedience to the Emperor's edict to appear and offer sacrifice, multitudes of Christians rushed to the forum in every city—some induced by fear of confiscation, some by a wish to retain offices in the public service, some by dread of tortures, some by the entreaties of friends and kindred; it seemed, says S. Cyprian, as if they had long been eager to find an opportunity of disowning their faith. The persecution was especially directed against the bishops and clergy. The chief object however was not to inflict death on the Christians but to force them to a recantation; with this view they were subjected to tortures, imprisonment, and want of food; and under such trials, the constancy of many gave way. The violence of the persecution did not last much over a year; for at the end of the year 251, Decius was killed in battle with the Goths.

inauditum, quid novum venerat ut velut incognitis, atque inopinatis rebus exortis, Christi sacramentum temeritate præcipiti solveretur? etc.

Cyprian, de Lapsis, 7: Ac multis proprius interitus satis non fuit: hortamentis mutuis, sin exitum suum populus impulsus est; mors invicem letali poculo propinata est.

[1] Origen. in Josu. Hom. VII. 6: Nolite divinis mundana miscere, nolite negotia seculi ecclesiæ secretis inserere.

Hoc modo accidit, quando sacerdotes qui populo præsunt erga delinquentes benigni volunt videri, et verentes peccantium linguas ne forte male de eis loquantur sacerdotalis severitatis immemores, nolunt implere quod scriptum est. Peccantem coram omnibus argue ut cæteri timorem habeant.

Cyprian, it appears[1], was elected to the vacant see of Carthage three years after his conversion, in the year 248, when he was 48 years of age, and he entered on his episcopate with an earnest resolution to correct the abuses and disorders which he found prevailing among his flock : but after two years, his labours for this purpose were interrupted by the persecution under Decius. The heathen populace clamoured that he should be thrown to the lions, and Cyprian withdrew to a retreat at no great distance for about 14 months. Besides those who actually sacrificed to the heathen gods, multitudes, by a payment to the magistrates, obtained certificates of having obeyed the Emperor's commands ; and many of these, who were called 'libellatics,' persuaded themselves that they had done nothing wrong. The troubles of the Carthaginian Church were increased by a practice which originated in the high regard entertained for martyrs and confessors. From a natural feeling of respect for those who shed their blood for the faith, martyrs had been allowed, perhaps as early as the middle of the 2nd century, to recommend for favourable consideration the cases of persons who were under ecclesiastical censure. Tickets were made out in such a form as to be available, not only for the person named in them, but for an indefinite number of others ; indulgences of this kind were distributed without limit, and even became a matter of traffic. Cyprian, from his retreat, kept up a constant communication with his Church, and endeavoured to check these disorders. A short time after Easter A.D. 251 the bishop returned to his city and held a Council on the subject of the Lapsed. It was agreed that such libel-

[1] Robertson's Church History, Vol. I. p. 116.

latics as had been penitent should be forthwith admitted to communion, and that those who had sacrificed should be allowed to hope for admission after a longer period of penance.

Certain lapsed persons had obtained from martyrs or confessors letters for their restitution to Church fellowship and presumed on them as superseding the necessity of anything more. Cyprian protests against the notion that such men's sins are pardoned before they had gone through the discipline required by the Church for the sin, as committed against it, and the method ordained by God for the sin as committed against Himself.

The following is a translation by N. Marshall, London 1717: [1]Let none impose upon nor deceive themselves, no man's pity can here avail them. No one can pardon the sins committed against God, but He alone who bare our sins, who suffered for our sakes, and whom God delivered up for our offences. It is impossible that man should be greater than God or equal to Him; nor is it therefore within the power of man, who is the servant, to forgive in any case a sin of so deep a dye as this, which is committed against our common Lord and Master; and the unhappy offender, who should in this case expect it,

---

[1] Cyprian, de Lapsis, § 11: Nemo se fallat, nemo se decipiat solus dominus misereri potest. Veniam peccatis, quæ in ipsum commissa sunt, solus potest ille largiri, qui peccata nostra portavit, qui pro nobis doluit, quem Deus tradidit pro peccatis nostris. Homo Deo esse non potest major: nec remittere aut donare indulgentia sua servus potest, quod in Dominum delicto graviore, commissum est: ne adhuc lapso et hoc accedat ad crimen, si nesciat esse predictum: Maledictus homo qui spem habet in homine. Dominus orandus est, Dominus nostra satisfactione placandus est, qui negantem negare se dixit, qui omne judicium de patre solus accepit.

would only add to his other misfortune the curse
denounced by God against such as should "trust in man."
Our Lord alone is here to be the object of his prayer,
He alone is to be pacified by the penitent's humiliation ;
He who has peremptorily declared that He will "deny
those who deny Him" and who hath received "all judgment from the Father."

S. Cyprian commends the practice of voluntary
confession where there was only an intention of
'apostasy,' although it never really occurred in fact.
[1]"How much more doth it argue of their faith and fear
of God ; who though guilty neither of sacrificing nor of
procuring certificates to indemnify them, yet because they
once had it in their thought and purpose, are desirous of
making their solemn acknowledgments to God and to his
Church of unburdening their consciences, and thus of
healing even the smallest wound inflicted by their
adversary : he remembering well that it is written 'God
is not mocked.'"

In three of his Epistles[2], the same Father allows the
confession of the lapsed to be received on the death-bed
preparatory to the imposition of hands ; but this was
only to meet the emergency of sudden illness overtaking
penitents : it was no part of a systematic practice.

S. Cyprian describes 'exomologesis' as a public be-

---

[1] Cyprian, de Lapsis, § 23 : Denique quanto et fide majores, et
timore meliores sunt, qui quamvis nullo sacrificii aut libelli facinore
constricti, quoniam tamen de hoc vel cogitaverunt, hoc ipsum apud
sacerdotes Dei dolenter et simpliciter confitentes Exhomologesin con-
scientiæ faciunt, animi sui pondus exponunt, salutarem medelam parvis
licet et modicis vulneribus exquirunt, scientes scriptum esse 'Deus non
deridetur.'

[2] Cyprian, Ep. 18—20.

wailing of sins and sharing in public penance by those
who had been less guilty than others, upon which
Albaspinæus[1] observes that the disburdening the load of
their mind means, not that they deposited their sins in
the hand of the priests but that through repentance and
exomologesis they freed the conscience from scruple,
and the burthen of having offended God by their
thoughts.

In an Epistle written by Cyprian[2] to martyrs and
confessors, who had given letters recommending certain
lapsed persons to be again received as members of the
Church, he writes in terms of complaint thus—"Certain
presbyters disregarding the law of the Gospel and also
your modest petition, before any submission to penitential discipline, before any confession of their very
weighty and crying sin, before any imposition of hands
by the bishop and his clergy, in order to their penance,
presume to make oblations for the lapsed and to admit
them to the Holy Eucharist, that is to profane the sacred
body of our Lord, since it is written 'Whosoever shall
eat the bread or drink the cup of the Lord unworthily,
shall be guilty of the Body and Blood of the Lord.'"

We here learn the course that Cyprian considered

---

[1] Note L on Tertullian, p. 378.

*Albaspinæus, notes on S. Cyprian, de Laps. c. 18, p. 171.

[2] Cyprian, Ep. xi. ad martyres et confessores qui lapsis petierant
pacem dari.

Illi (presbyteri) contra Evangelii legem, contra vestram quoque
honorificam petitionem, ante actam pœnitentiam, ante exhomologesin
gravissimi atque extremi delicti factam, ante manum ab Episcopo et
clero in pœnitentiam impositam, offerre lapsis pacem et Eucharistiam
dare, id est sanctum Domini corpus profanare audeant, cum scriptum
sit: Qui ederit panem, aut biberit calicem Domini indigne, reus erit
corporis et sanguinis Domini.

to be necessary for those who had denied the Christian A.D. 300
Faith in the time of the Decian persecution before they
were readmitted to the communion of the Church.

To the same effect he writes to his lay-brethren who
remained true to the faith.

[1] "For if in offences of a less heinous dye, which
are not directly committed against our Lord, there be a
confessed necessity of submitting to public penance for a
certain season, and of acknowledging the sin in a very
solemn manner, and of inspecting the life and conversation
of the person under discipline; and if no one can be
received, even in these lower cases, to communion,
without imposition of hands by the bishop and his clergy;
how much more necessary is all this, in the case of these
more enormous and grievous sins."

We may here observe that the case of those, who
through *fear* forsook the Christian religion, and afterwards desired to be re-admitted to its privileges, was
that which chiefly employed the discipline of the first
three centuries.

Summary of the practice of Confession during these first three centuries.

We gather from the evidence within our reach that
during this period up to the end of the 3rd century

---

[1] Cyprian, Ep. XII. ad plebem de rescripto Martyrum ac iis qui
pacem petebant.

Nam cum in minoribus delictis, quæ non in dominum committuntur,
pœnitentia agatur justo tempore et exhomologesis fiat inspecta vita ejus,
qui agit pœnitentiam, nec ad communicationem venire quis possit, nisi
prius illi ab episcopo et clero manus fuerit imposita: quanto magis in
his gravissimis ex extremis delictis caute omnia et moderate secundum
disciplinam Domini observari oportet.

the confessions (of those who became members of the Church) were in the first instance those of converts or of the catechumens seeking baptism, who were required to acknowledge the evil of their former lives and to make open declaration of their conversion to the Christian Faith and of their belief in Jesus Christ as their Redeemer. After being enrolled as members of the Church, if they were guilty of any great and scandalous sin, and the Church gained knowledge of it, either after public condemnation or by self-accusation to the bishop or chief pastors of the Church, they were required to make a solemn confession before the congregation, provided their so doing would not render them liable to death either through the civil courts or by personal revenge ; then they had to submit to a course of humiliation and prayer, groaning and lamenting over their sin, they were shut out from the privileges of the services and communion of the Church, until by their outward signs of sorrow it was judged that their repentance was sincere and their amendment of life assured. The prayers of the bishop and congregation were offered up on their behalf, beseeching God to pardon the offenders, and after imposition of hands by the bishop they were re-admitted to their former position among the members of the congregation. There were instances, as we learn from Origen, of some persons who had misgivings as to their conduct and were anxious to receive counsel from those more skilled in the knowledge of Christ : these sought some sympathetic and discreet minister to whom they could unburden their conscience and receive advice, even when their irregularity of thought and action did not deserve the weighty censure of the Church.

CHAPTER III.

EARLY in the 4th century, Peter of Alexandria[1], like A.D. 320 Origen, recommends confession to a priest as part of the means of securing pardon, though it is the penitent then who with amendment and almsgiving cures himself, and not the priest that cures him, so that it was merely a wholesome exercise.

Lactantius[2], who died before the Council of Nicæa, A.D. 325, speaking against obstinate offenders, alludes to confession as part of the *act* of penance. " God, willing in His everlasting loving-kindness to provide for our life and salvation, set forth to us penance, that if we cleanse our heart, *i.e.* if confessing our sin, we make amends to God, we may obtain pardon which to the contumacious and to such as conceal their sin is denied by Him, who

---

[1] Dr Lea, Auricular Confession and Indulgences, Vol. I. p. 176. *Deinde per confessionem peccatum suum sacerdoti manifestans nitens in contrarium, eleemosynas scilicet faciens curabit infirmitatem. Palmieri, Tract. de Pœn. p. 366.

[2] Lactantius, IV. 17 : Volens enim vitæ ac saluti nostræ pro æterna sua pietate consulere, pœnitentiam nobis in illa circumcisione proposuit, ut si cor nudaverimus, id est, si peccata nostra confessi satis Deo fecerimus, veniam consequamur; quæ contumacibus et admissa sua celantibus denegatur ab eo qui non faciem sicut homo sed intima et arcana pectoris intuetur.

not as man seeth the face, but the inmost secrets of the heart."

S. Anthony[1], who lived A.D. 251—355, directs his fellow-recluses that they should write down their thoughts and actions, and exhibit the record to one another; which probably was *the beginning of habitual confession* among monastic orders, where there are many grounds for supposing it prevailed long before it became the custom of the Church.

In Athanasius' account[2] of the death of Anthony there is no allusion to a previous confession, and we may fairly assume that confession immediately before death was not customary with the saints and fathers of the early Church or we should find mention made of it in the records of their death.

In the time of Basil, who was Bishop of Cæsarea about A.D. 370 (as stated on p. 48), a priest had been specially appointed in each diocese whose office it was to receive private confessions and decide whether the sins should be openly acknowledged before the congregation. Basil directs that in cases of doubts and difficulty resort should be had to a priest. The regulations to be observed show that private confession was a frequent practice, but still the confession was with a view to public penance and the 'penitentiary' determined what and how much of the confession should be before the congregation.

[3]Now there were two sets of persons who were subjected to public penance—" such persons as stood *convicted* of notorious sin " and " those who, having been

---

[1] *Athanasius, Vita Anth. Erem. p. 75.

[2] *Athanasius, Vita Anth. Erem.

[3] Dr Pusey's Preface to Gaume's Manual for Confessors, p. xlvi.

guilty of the same sins, but whose sins were hid from all A.D. 370
eyes saving the all-seeing eye of God, driven by their
own consciences, confessed them and were subject to the
same course of penitence." These last then only openly
confessed such sins before the congregation as the penitentiary recommended after the matter had been disclosed
to him. Some of such sins were therefore not openly
confessed before the congregation, though the sinner might
be subjected to public penitence.

[1]The Fathers did not command that publication
should be made of the guilt of women who had been
adulteresses, and who out of godly fear confessed or were
anyhow convicted, lest an open confession should give
occasion of death to them, being convicted in a civil
court, but commanded that they should be placed without
communion until the time of penitence was fulfilled.

The stations in Church of penitents.

It may be interesting to insert here Basil's description
of the different stations of penitents in his time, the
middle of the 4th century.

[2]"Of such as offended by 'incontinence' who for

---

[1] S. Basil, Ep. CXCIX. Can. 34: Τὰς μοιχευθείσας γυναῖκας καὶ
ἐξαγορευούσας δι' εὐλάβειαν, ἢ ὁπωσοῦν ἐλεγχομένας, δημοσιεύειν οὐκ
ἐκέλευσαν οἱ πατέρες ἡμῶν, ἵνα μὴ θανάτου αἰτίαν παράσχωμεν ἐλεγ-
χθείσαις· ἵστασθαι δὲ αὐτὰς ἄνευ κοινωνίας προσέταξαν, μέχρι τοῦ συμπλη-
ροῦσθαι τὸν χρόνον τῆς μετανοίας. Similar precautions are laid down by
Origen and Augustine.

[2] Basil in Epist. Canonic. ad Amphilochium Iconii Episcop. Ep.
199: Ἔστι δὲ ἐν τέσσαρσιν ἔτεσιν ὡρισμένη τοῖς πορνεύουσιν, ἡ ἐπιτίμησις·
χρὴ δὲ τῷ πρώτῳ ἐκβάλλεσθαι τῶν προσευχῶν, καὶ προσκλαίειν αὐτοὺς τῇ
θύρᾳ τῆς ἐκκλησίας· τῷ δευτέρῳ δεχθῆναι εἰς ἀκρόασιν· τῷ τρίτῳ εἰς
μετάνοιαν· τῷ τετάρτῳ εἰς σύστασιν μετὰ τοῦ λαοῦ, ἀπεχομένους τῆς
προσφορᾶς· εἶτα αὐτοῖς ἐπιτρέπεσθαι τὴν κοινωνίαν τοῦ ἀγαθοῦ.

the first year were to be excluded entirely from the
whole service, and to stand weeping at the Church door,
which was the station of mourners; in the year following,
they were admitted to that of hearers; in the third to
that of the prostrate, called by way of eminence 'the
penance'; in the fourth, they were permitted to stand
with the faithful whilst they communicated, but might
not themselves partake with them." And this has been
termed by some writers the station of 'by-standers';
and thus at last they were restored in full to all their
privileges and were allowed to communicate.

About A.D. 360, S. Hilary of Poitiers[1] declares the
sufficiency and necessity of confession to God for the
pardon of sin.

Basil[2] gives certain directions in the form of 'question
and answer'; thus he proposes (q. 229) "whether forbidden actions ought to be laid open to all, or to whom,
and of what sort," and he adds the answer "that as with
bodily sufferings, so also the discovery of sins ought to
be made to those able to cure them," and again he asks
(q. 288) whether "he who wishes to confess his sins
ought to confess them to all or to any chance person or

---

[1] Hilary on Ps. xxxi.: Iniquitati enim alia nulla medicina nisi confessio ad Deum.

[2] Basil, Reg. brev. tract.

Qn. 229.   Εἰ χρὴ τὰς ἀπηγορευμένας πράξεις ἀνεπαισχυντότερον·
            ἐξαγορεύειν πᾶσιν, ἢ τισί· καὶ ποίοις τούτοις;

Ans.   Ὡς οὖν τὰ πάθη τοῦ σώματος οὐ πᾶσιν ἀποκαλύπτουσιν οἱ
            ἄνθρωποι, οὔτε τοῖς τυχοῦσιν, ἀλλὰ τοῖς ἐμπείροις τῆς
            τούτων θεραπείας.

Qn. 288.   Ὁ θέλων ἐξομολογήσασθαι τὰς ἁμαρτίας ἑαυτοῦ εἰ πᾶσιν
            ἐξομολογεῖσθαι ὀφείλει, καὶ τοῖς τυχοῦσιν, ἢ τισίν;

Ans.   Ἀναγκαῖον τοῖς πεπιστευμένοις τὴν οἰκονομίαν τῶν μυστη-
            ρίων τοῦ Θεοῦ ἐξομολογεῖσθαι τὰ ἁμαρτήματα.

to whom?" and he replies "it is necessary to confess
them to those entrusted with the oracles of God." There
would have been no necessity for regulations like these
had private confession been in frequent practice.

Monks are directed by a rule, similar to that of
Anthony, to tell to the common body any 'thought of
things forbidden, or unsuitable words or remissness in
prayer or luke-warmness in psalmody, or desire after
ordinary life,' "that through the common prayers the evil
may be cured"; and also "on referring everything, even
the secrets of the heart, to the superior."

Confession to the priest in private was at this time in use.

Gregory of Nyssa, in the case of those who are led A.D. 370
into sin by the allurements of pleasure, speaks of secret
confession, which is to be followed by penance, [1] "he
who of his own accord advances to the discovery of his
sins, as by his voluntary accusation of himself, he gives a
specimen of the change that is in his mind towards that
which is good, will deserve lighter correction," alluding
to the well established rule that voluntary confession was
allowed to mitigate the subsequent penance; and in
another place he writes as if he commended the custom
of confessing all transgression of positive law, whether it

Smith's Dictionary of Christian Antiquities &c. 'exomologesis.'
Quoted also by Marshall, Pen. Disc. p. 190.

[1] Gregory of Nyssa Ep. ad Letoiim: Ὁ μὲν γὰρ ἀφ' ἑαυτοῦ πρὸς
τὴν ἐξαγόρευσιν τῆς ἁμαρτίας ὁρμήσας, αὐτῷ τὸ καταδείξασθαι δι' οἰκείας
ὁρμῆς γενέσθαι τῶν κρυφίων κατήγορος· ὡς ἤδη τῆς θεραπείας τοῦ πάθους
ἀρξάμενος, καὶ σημεῖον τῆς πρὸς τὸ κρεῖττον μεταβολῆς ἐπιδειξάμενος, ἐν
φιλανθρωποτέροις γίνεται τοῖς ἐπιτιμίοις.

involved penance or not, [1]"if he who has transferred to himself the property of another by secret theft, shall unfold his offence by secret confession, it will be sufficient to cure the guilt by a contrary disposition, *i.e.* by liberal alms to weed out that covetous humour which led him into his sin."

A.D. 382　　S. Chrysostom speaks of the great authority and dignity of the Priesthood, but nowhere speaks of Confession to a Priest as incumbent on a sinner, but [2]alludes to the grief and concern the Bishop must be under, when he is obliged to cut off a member from the ' Communion of the Church.'

He speaks of the honour the Holy Spirit has vouchsafed to His Priests, and of the power which God has conferred upon them, saying, Whatsoever ye shall bind on earth shall be bound in heaven, and whatsoever ye shall loose on earth, shall be loosed in heaven. [3]" That

---

[1] Gregory of Nyssa Ep. ad Letoiim : Ὁ δὲ δι' ὑφαιρέσεως λανθανούσης σφετεριζόμενος τὸ ἀλλότριον, εἶτα δι' ἐξαγορεύσεως τὸ πλημμέλημα αὐτοῦ τῷ ἱερεῖ φανερώσας, τῇ περὶ τὸ ἐναντίον τοῦ πάθους σπουδῇ θεραπεύσει τὴν ἀρρωστίαν. λέγω δὲ διὰ τοῦ τὰ προσόντα παρέχειν τοῖς πένησιν, ἵνα τῷ προέσθαι ἃ ἔχει, φανερὸς γένηται καθαρεύων τῆς κατὰ πλεονεξίαν νόσου.

[2] S. Chrysostom de Sacerdotio. Lib. III. 18: Τί ἄν τις λέγοι τὰς λύπας, ἃς ὑπομένουσιν, ἡνίκα ἂν δέῃ τινὰ τοῦ τῆς Ἐκκλησίας περικόψαι πληρώματος.

[3] S. Chrysostom de Sacerdotio, Lib. III. 5 : καὶ ἅπερ ἂν ἐργάσωνται κάτω οἱ ἱερεῖς, ταῦτα ὁ Θεὸς ἄνω κυροῖ, καὶ τὴν τῶν δούλων γνώμην ὁ Δεσπότης βεβαιοῖ. Καὶ τί γὰρ ἀλλ' ἢ πᾶσαν αὐτοῖς τὴν οὐράνιον ἔδωκεν ἐξουσίαν; Ὧν γὰρ ἂν, φησὶν, ἀφῆτε τὰς ἁμαρτίας, ἀφέωνται, καὶ ὧν ἂν κρατῆτε, κεκράτηνται......Εἰ γὰρ οὐ δύναταί τις εἰσελθεῖν εἰς τὴν βασιλείαν τῶν οὐρανῶν, ἐὰν μὴ δι' ὕδατος καὶ πνεύματος ἀναγεννηθῇ καὶ ὁ μὴ τρώγων τὴν σάρκα τοῦ Κυρίου, καὶ τὸ αἷμα αὐτοῦ πίνων, ἐκβέβληται τῆς αἰωνίου ζωῆς, πάντα δὲ ταῦτα δι' ἑτέρου μὲν οὐδενός, μόνον δὲ διὰ τῶν ἁγίων ἐκείνων ἐπιτελεῖται χειρῶν, τῶν τοῦ ἱερέως λέγω· πῶς ἄν τις, τούτων ἐκτὸς, ἢ τὸ τῆς γεέννης ἐκφυγεῖν δυνήσεται πῦρ, ἢ τῶν ἀποκειμένων στεφάνων τυχεῖν;

what is done by His Priests below is confirmed by God above : and the Lord ratifies the sentence of His servants. He tells them 'Whosesoever sins ye remit, they are remitted unto them, and whosesoever sins ye retain, they are retained.'" From this he points out the power conferred on Priests, the dignity of their order, for without them by whom the Sacraments of Baptism and the Eucharist are administered, no man can escape the flames of Hell or obtain the promised Crowns of Reward.

He goes on to speak of the power of Priests[1], "who have often saved sick souls, when they were upon the brink of eternal destruction : inflicting upon some a milder punishment, and keeping others from falling. And this not only by doctrine and instruction, but by the assistance of their prayers; for by them we are regenerated into a state of grace, and by their pardon are restored to it."

Even with these high views of the priesthood he recommends confession of sins to God alone, as in the following passages of his writings, some of many to the same distinct evidence. He represents God as saying to the sinner[2] "I compel thee not," He saith, "to come

---

[1] S. Chrysostom de Sacerdotio, Lib. III. 6: Οὗτοι δὲ καὶ κάμνουσαν καὶ ἀπόλλυσθαι μέλλουσαν τὴν ψυχὴν πολλάκις ἔσωσαν, τοῖς μὲν πραοτέραν τὴν κόλασιν ἐργασάμενοι, τοὺς δὲ οὐδὲ παρὰ τὴν ἀρχὴν ἀφέντες ἐμπεσεῖν, οὐ τῷ διδάσκειν μόνον καὶ νουθετεῖν, ἀλλὰ καὶ τῷ δι' εὐχῶν βοηθεῖν. Οὐ γὰρ ὅταν ἡμᾶς ἀναγεννῶσι μόνον, ἀλλὰ καὶ τὰ μετὰ ταῦτα συγχωρεῖν ἔχουσιν ἐξουσίαν ἁμαρτήματα.

[2] Chrysostom de Incomp. Hom. 5: Οὐδὲ γὰρ εἰς θέατρόν σε ἄγω τῶν συνδούλων τῶν σῶν, οὐδὲ ἐκκαλύψαι τοῖς ἀνθρώποις ἀναγκάζω τὰ ἁμαρτήματα· τὸ συνειδὸς ἀνάπτυξον ἔμπροσθεν τοῦ Θεοῦ, καὶ αὐτῷ δεῖξον τὰ τραύματα, καὶ παρ' αὐτοῦ τὰ φάρμακα αἴτησαι.

This passage has been considered such strong testimony in favour of

into the midst of a theatre, surrounded by many witnesses. Tell Me alone thy sin apart, that I may heal the sore, and free thee from the pain."

And again—"But thou art ashamed and blushest to utter thy sins; nay, but even if it were necessary to utter these things before men and display them, not even thus shouldest thou be ashamed: (for sin, not to confess sin, is shame), but now it is not even necessary to confess before witnesses." [1]"Be the examination of transgressions in the thoughts of conscience. Be the judgment-seat unwitnessed. Let God alone see thee confessing, who upbraideth not sins, but remitteth sins on confession."

So too he leaves it to one's own conscience as to fitness to receive the Holy Communion [2]. "If we do this (reconcile ourselves with the brethren) we shall be able with a pure conscience to approach this pure and awful table, and to utter boldly those words joined to our prayers—the initiated know what I mean. Wherefore I leave to every one's own conscience, how fulfilling that command we may at that fearful moment utter these things with boldness."

'confession to God alone' that it is quoted by Bingham, bk. VIII. c. III. § 2. Hooker, bk. VI. p. 52. Marshall's Pen. Disc. p. 37. Note M. Tertullian, p. 399. Maskell on Absolution, p. 173.

[1] Περὶ μετανοίας καὶ ἐξομολογήσεως παρὰ τοῖς λογισμοῖς γενέσθω τῶν πεπλημμελημένων ἡ ἐξέτασις, ἀμάρτυρον ἔστω τὸ δικαστήριον, ὁ Θεὸς ὁράτω μόνος ἐξομολογούμενον.

Smith's Dictionary of Christian Antiquities &c. "exomologesis."

[2] S. Chrysostom Hom. 27 in Gen., Migne LIII. p. 251: Ἂν τοῦτο κατορθώσωμεν, δυνησόμεθα μετὰ καθαροῦ συνειδότος καὶ τῇ ἱερᾷ ταύτῃ καὶ φρικτῇ τραπέζῃ προσελθεῖν, καὶ τὰ ῥήματα ἐκεῖνα τὰ τῇ εὐχῇ συνεζευγμένα μετὰ παρρησίας φθέγξασθαι. Ἴσασιν οἱ μεμνημένοι τὸ λεγόμενον. Διὸ τῷ ἑκάστου συνειδότι καταλιμπάνω εἰδέναι, πῶς μὲν κατωρθωκότες τὴν ἐντολὴν μετὰ παρρησίας προέσθαι ταῦτα δυνάμεθα κατὰ τὸν καιρὸν ἐκεῖνον τὸν φοβερόν.

S. Chrysostom[1] though he speaks of Confession to God, to a priest or before a congregation, certainly upholds Confession to God as the chief essential for securing pardon, and admits the performance of confession to a priest or before the congregation only as a means of quickening the conscience or improving the repentance of the sinner.

S. Ambrose, Archbishop of Milan, born A.D. 340, writes 40 years afterwards, speaking of Confession, and [2]recommends sinners to make acknowledgment of their sins unto God and by this means obtain pardon "if thou A.D. 380 wilt be justified, confess thine offence. For humble confession looses the bonds of sins," and not to remain among those wicked persons who increase their guilt by a pretended innocence and "make boast of their innocence and by justifying themselves are the more burthened." The same instruction is given us in the First Epistle of S. John[3], "If we say that we have no sin, we deceive ourselves, and the truth is not in us": "but if we confess our sins, he is faithful and just to forgive us our sins and to cleanse us from all unrighteousness." From these words we may safely conclude that it is

---

[1] S. Chrysostom in Ep. ad Hebræos Hom. XXXI. n. 3, quoted by Bingham, bk. XVIII. ch. III. § 2, and by Dr Lea, Vol. I. p. 180: Οὐ λέγω σοι, Ἐκπόμπευσον σαυτὸν, οὐδὲ παρὰ τοῖς ἄλλοις κατηγόρησον, ἀλλὰ πείθεσθαι συμβουλεύω τῷ προφήτῃ λέγοντι· Ἀποκάλυψον πρὸς Κύριον τὴν ὁδόν σου. Ἐπὶ τοῦ Θεοῦ ταῦτα ὁμολόγησον, ἐπὶ τοῦ δικαστοῦ ὁμολόγει τὰ ἁμαρτήματα, εὐχόμενος, εἰ καὶ μὴ τῇ γλώττῃ, ἀλλὰ τῇ μνήμῃ, καὶ οὕτως ἀξίου ἐλεηθῆναι. Ἅν ἔχῃς τὰ ἁμαρτήματα διηνεκῶς ἐν τῇ μνήμῃ, οὐδέποτε τῷ πλησίον μνησικακήσεις.

[2] S. Ambrose de Pæn. II. 6: Ne glorieris, quasi innocens ne te justificando plus ingraves. Si vis justificari, fatere delictum tuum. Solvit enim criminum nexus verecunda confessio peccatorum.

[3] 1 S. John i. 8, 9.

confession to God, who is able to justify, to forgive and to cleanse, which should be made by the sinner, and is directed by S. Ambrose without any allusion to confession to men.

The manner in which he comments on S. Peter's denial and repentance afterwards is inconsistent with the existence of a custom of private confession in his time. Thus[1], "Let tears wash away the guilt which one is afraid to confess with the voice. Tears express the fault without alarm; tears confess the sin without injuring bashfulness; tears obtain the pardon they ask not for." [2]"Peter wept most bitterly, that with tears he might wash away his offence. Do thou also, if thou wouldest obtain pardon, wash out thy fault with tears." And applying the penitence of S. Peter to ourselves, he adds[3], "I find not what he said, I find that he wept, I read of his tears, I read not of his excusing himself, but what cannot be excused can be washed away."

Another passage, by the same Father, selected by [4]Bellarmine, manifestly relates to the course of discipline

---

[1] S. Ambrose on Luke, Lib. x. § 88: Lavant lachrymæ delictum, quod pudor est voce confiteri. Et veniæ fletus consulunt et verecundiæ. Lachrymæ sine horrore culpam loquuntur; lachrymæ crimen sine offensione verecundiæ confitentur; lachrymæ veniam non postulant, et merentur.......

[2] § 90. Flevit ergo et amarissime Petrus, flevit ut lachrymis suum posset lavare delictum: et tu, si veniam vis mereri, dilue lachrymis culpam tuam.

[3] S. Ambrose, Lib. x. § 88: Non invenio quid dixerit Petrus; invenio quod fleverit, Lachrymas ejus lego: satisfactionem ejus non lego. Quoted by Gratian Tract. de Pæn. qu. III. distinctio I; also by Bingham, bk. XVIII. ch. III. § 2.

[4] Bellarmine de Pæn. Lib. III. ch. 8: Habemus sanctum Ambrosium, qui libro secundo de pænitentia capite sexto, sic ait "Si vis justificari, fatere delictum tuum: solvit enim criminum nexus verecunda

and refers to those who had made confession of their sin to the priest charged with receiving such confession, and who then determined the amount of penance to be imposed. It appears that many, having taken the first step of confession owing to a qualm of conscience, shrank from the performance of the penance assigned owing to their fear of the exposure before their brethren. And so S. Ambrose writes that "very many out of fear of future punishment, conscious of their own sins, seek admission to penitence, and having obtained it, are drawn back by the shame of public entreaty." And he adds, "Can any one believe that you would be ashamed to plead with God for pardon, from whom thou art not hid, when thou art not ashamed to confess thy sins to man from whom thou art hid?"

When S. Basil speaks of the necessity "to confess the sins to those entrusted with the oracles of God" he evidently considered confession should be made to the Penitentiary that he might advise whether the sins were to be openly confessed before the congregation or no, as was then the known discipline of the Greek Church.

S. Basil informs us that it was the practice of the Eastern Church in his time that the people all confessed their sins with great contrition at the beginning of the Nocturnal Service and before the Psalmody and Lessons

confessio peccatorum"; et capite nono scribit "multos fuisse, qui libenter confitebantur privatim sacerdotibus, sed publice in Ecclesia satisfacere recusabant": "plerique" inquit "futuri supplicii metu peccatorum suorum conscii pænitentiam petunt: et cum acceperint, publicæ supplicationis revocantur pudore"; et capite decimo "An quisquam ferat, ut erubescas Deum rogare, qui non erubescis rogare hominem? et pudeat te Deo supplicare, quem non lates; cum non pudeat peccata tua homini, quem lateas, confiteri?"

commenced. This fact is quoted by Palmer[1] in his Origines Liturgicæ in justification of the position of the General Confession of our Morning and Evening Service.

This Father tells us that he himself only made his confession to God, saying[2], "I do not make confession with my lips to appear to the world, but inwardly in my heart, where no eye sees; I declare my groanings unto Thee alone 'who seest in secret.' I roar within myself for I need not many words to make confession, the groanings of my heart are sufficient for confession, and the lamentations, which are sent up to Thee, my God, from the bottom of my soul."

It appears moreover that [3]according to the practice of the Church in the 4th century there was a general and daily confession of sins of lesser degree, to God at the ordinary night service, described by S. Basil. "Among us the people go at night to the house of prayer and in distress, affliction, and continual tears, make confession to God. At last they rise from their prayers and begin to sing psalms......and so, after passing the night in various psalmody, praying at intervals as the day begins to dawn, all together as with one voice and one heart raise the Psalm of Confession (Ps. LI) to the Lord."

The same author, Dr Swete, tells us that the writer

---

[1] Palmer, Origines Liturgicæ, Vol. I. p. 240.

[2] S. Basil in Ps. xxxvii. 8: Οὐ γὰρ ἵνα τοῖς πολλοῖς φανερὸς γένωμαι, τοῖς χείλεσιν ἐξομολογοῦμαι· ἔνδον δὲ ἐν αὐτῇ τῇ καρδίᾳ, τὸ ὄμμα μύων, σοὶ μόνῳ τῷ βλέποντι τὰ ἐν κρυπτῷ τοὺς ἐμαυτοῦ στεναγμοὺς ἐπιδεικνύω, ἐν ἐμαυτῷ ὠρυόμενος. Οὐδὲ γὰρ μακρῶν μοι λόγων χρεία ἦν πρὸς τὴν ἐξομολόγησιν· ἀπήρκουν γὰρ οἱ στεναγμοὶ τῆς καρδίας μου πρὸς ἐξομολό-γησιν, καὶ οἱ ἀπὸ βάθους ψυχῆς πρὸς σὲ τὸν Θεὸν ἀναπεμπόμενοι ὀδυρμοί.

[3] Church Services by Dr H. B. Swete, pp. 34, 35.

of the Tract on "Virginity," attributed to Athanasius, directs "the Virgin, whether alone or in company with others, to rise at night and repeat the fifty-first Psalm and as many others as can be said standing, following by confession and prayer, with an Alleluia after every third." This evidently shows that there was to be a recounting of daily sin to God with a view of creating a sorrow in the heart and a true feeling of repentance and a desire of forgiveness. This daily exercise would naturally check sin and lead the sinner to a better and holier life.

The [1]Council of Laodicea A.D. 372, speaking of the A.D. 372 whole course of penance to which the sinner is required to conform, says "as to those who sin by divers offences and persevere in the prayer of confession and repentance, and turn perfectly from the evil ways, a period of repentance being assigned to such, proportioned to the offence, let them be admitted to Communion through the mercies and goodness of God."

About this period we meet with three forms of voluntary confession in more or less frequent use—confession to God, to the congregation gathered in the Church, and to a priest or some other holy man. S. Ambrose supplies us with evidence of each of them[2].

---

[1] Council of Laodicea, Can. 2: Omnes qui peccarunt, qualiacunque dicat aliquis eorum peccata, si pænitentiam egerint, et ea confessi fuerint, et a malis perfecte se converterint, et tempus ad pænitentiam agendum secundum delicti proportionem iis concessum precibus et lacrymis absolverint, propter Dei miserationes et bonitatem in communionem recipientur.

[2] S. Ambrose de Pæn. bk. II. ch. 5: Et nos ergo non erubescamus fateri Domino peccata nostra.

id. ch. 53: Novit omnia Dominus sed expectat vocem tuam; non ut puniat sed ut ignoscat.

id. ch. 91: Hoc ergo in Ecclesia facere fastidis ut Deo supplices, ut

He speaks of confession to God as a means of setting
the heart right towards God, the ordinary and recognized
practice of those struck with remorse for their sin, who
sincerely seek God's pardon. He also points out the
method of reconciling the sinner with the Church, he
points out the weighty nature of its censure, and endeavours to persuade penitents to lay aside a feeling of shame
in making their confession in the Church, whereby they
may obtain the prayers of the brethen in their behalf.
He thus shows that this public confession was voluntary
and for secret sins : this, he says, procures admission to
the Sacrament, which removes the sin, so that he considered that a due receiving of the Holy Communion
secured pardon, and that, by a course of penance, the
sinner only received a removal of the censure of the
Church which his sin had procured for him. At the
same time we learn that [1] he showed the greatest sympathy
with those who sought him privately to confess their
sins to him, but he never ventured to do more than
intercede for them with God and advise them to practise
humiliation before God and an abstaining from sin. He
makes no mention of any necessity of the penitent to
reveal his sin to him or to any other priest of the Church,

patrocinium tibi ad obsecrandum sanctæ plebis requiras, ubi nihil est
quod pudori esse debeat, nisi non fateri, cum omnes simus peccatores.

[1] Paulinus, Vita S. Ambros. ch. 39: Erat etiam gaudens cum
gaudentibus et flens cum flentibus ; si quidem quotiescumque illi aliquis
ob percipiendam pœnitentiam lapsus suos confessus esset, ita flebat ut et
illum flere compelleret ; videbatur enim sibi cum jacente jacere. Causas
autem criminum quæ illi confitebatur, nulli nisi Domino soli, apud
quem intercedebat, loquebatur; bonum relinquens exemplum posteris
sacerdotibus ut intercessores apud Deum magis sint quam accusatores
apud homines.

neither does he presume to pronounce any form of Absolution; but he deals with the sinner who has confided in him with fatherly love and gives him advice as to his future conduct. Such a practice of seeking counsel from one holding a position of authority in the Church could not but be permitted though not directed. The sinner would doubtless thus obtain assistance in gaining for himself reconciliation to God: but at this time the formularies of the Church were drawn up only in reference to public confession. S. Ambrose himself knows [1] only of public penance for grave sins: the venial sins of daily occurrence were removed by repentance and prayer. The confessor had no power to do anything but to pray and advise as indicated by Origen. If reconciliation with the Church were wanted, the sin secretly confessed had to be published to the congregation in order that public penance might be imposed, but this [2] rule, as we have mentioned before, was relaxed in the case of women guilty of adultery, lest it should lead to their death, though they were suspended from Communion for the period assigned by the Canons.

When Nectarius was Patriarch of Constantinople A.D. 390 A.D. 381—397 a [3] terrible scandal arose in the Church

---

[1] S. Ambrose de Pæn. lib. II. ch. 95: Nam si vero agerent pænitentiam, iterandam postea non putarent: quia sicut unum baptisma, ita una pænitentia, quæ tamen publice agitur; nam quotidiani nos debet pænitere peccati; sed hæc delictorum leviorum, illa graviorum.

[2] S. Basil, Epist. Canon. CXCIX. 34, quoted on p. 47.

[3] Sozomen, Hist. Eccles. lib. VII. ch. 16: Ἐν δὲ τῇ Κωνσταντινου-πόλει Ἐκκλησίᾳ, ὁ ἐπὶ τῶν μετανοούντων τεταγμένος πρεσβύτερος ἐπολί-τεύετο. Εἰσότε δὴ γυνή τις τῶν εὐπατριδῶν, ἐπὶ ἁμαρτίαις αἷς προσήγγειλε, προσταχθεῖσα παρὰ τούτου τοῦ πρεσβυτέρου νηστεύειν, καὶ τὸν Θεὸν ἱκετεύειν, τούτου χάριν ἐν τῇ ἐκκλησίᾳ διατρίβουσα, ἐκπεπορνεῦσθαι παρ' ἀνδρὸς διακόνου κατεμήνυσεν. Ἐφ' ᾧ τὸ πλῆθος μαθόν, ἐχαλέπαινεν ὡς τῆς ἐκκλησίας ὑβρισμένης. Μεγίστη δὲ διαβολὴ τοὺς ἱερωμένους εἶχεν.

owing to a misunderstanding or to the indiscreet advice of the Penitentiary. The members of the Church were greatly distressed at the open confession by a lady of good position of her intimacy with a Deacon of the Church. Thereupon A.D. 391 Nectarius abolished the office of Penitentiary in the Eastern Church, and we do not hear of this office having ever existed in the West. Almost all the Bishops in the East followed the example of Nectarius.

[1] As long as public voluntary confession of private crimes did continue in either branch of the Church, the Latin or the Greek, as in the one it remained not much above 200 years, in the other about 400, the only acts of such Repentance were ; first, the offender's intimation of those crimes to some one Presbyter, for which imposition of Penance was sought ; secondly, the undertaking of Penance, imposed by the Bishop ; thirdly, after the same, performed and ended, open confession to God in the hearing of the whole Church ; whereupon, fourthly, ensued the Prayer of the Church ; fifthly, then the Bishop's imposition of hands ; and so, sixthly, the party's reconciliation or restitution to his former right in the Holy Sacrament.

The only[2] crimes which the Church took notice of during the first four centuries seem to have been, (i) idolatry or heresy, (ii) homicide, and (iii) unchastity :

Ἀπορῶν δὲ ὅ τι χρήσαιτο τῷ συμβεβηκότι Νεκτάριος, ἀφείλετο τῆς διακονίας τὸν ἡταιρηκότα. Συμβουλευσάντων δέ τινων συγχωρεῖν ἕκαστον, ὡς ἂν ἑαυτῷ συνειδείη καὶ θαῤῥεῖν δύναιτο, κοινωνεῖν τῶν μυστηρίων, ἔπαυσε τὸν ἐπὶ τῆς μετανοίας πρεσβύτερον.

Dr Pusey, Gaume, p. xlviii.

[1] Hooker's Eccles. Pol. bk. VI. p. 43.

[2] Acts xv. 28, 29.

these point to the *three* great branches of duty towards God, our neighbour, and ourselves.

S. Augustine held the Bishoprick of Hippo from A.D. 395 to 430: here he found that the Donatists were in a great majority, and with a view of maintaining the general discipline, he proposed, when a person, who was under censure of either community, applied for admission into the other, it should not be granted, except on condition of his submitting to penance, which rule he himself scrupulously observed.

Summary of the Practice of Confession during the 4th Century.

Up to the end of the 4th century, we gather from the above evidence that Confession among Christians, after they were once admitted by Baptism to membership of the Christian community, at first consisted in making open confession before the congregation of sins of a gross character ; and the Bishop or chief Priest of such Church acted as minister on the part of the congregation for receiving this open confession, for conducting the penitent through the different stages of penance, whereby the genuineness of the sorrow declared, and the promise of amendment might be realized : and then after the prayers of the congregation were offered up on the sinner's behalf, followed the re-admission of the sinner by the laying on of hands. Inconvenience was found to arise from the indiscriminate publication of all scandalous sins, and the Bishops found that the burden to them was too great, and as the Church grew they sought some relief from this unpleasant duty. Thus there arose a system of confessing privately in the first instance, either to a priest who was deemed discreet and of a specially holy life, or to a priest who, as time went on, was absolutely appointed for the purpose; and if in either case it was determined by such priest necessary or even desirable that open Confession should be made before the congregation, this had to be done as the first step towards the re-admission of such an offender to the full privileges of membership. Such sins as it was thought undesirable to confess openly, required the prayers of the penitent and of the priest for God's pardon, and when real repentance for the sin was manifest, the sinner was allowed to resume his place among the faithful. People naturally felt ashamed to make public acknowledgment of their sins, though they felt an ease to their distress in finding some one in whom they could confide, and when the office of Penitentiary was abolished towards the end of the 4th century, less searching out of offenders crept in: sinners were left more to themselves—notorious sins still demanded a course of humiliation and penance by the offenders—secret sins were still kept secret even though the sinner might be seen in the Church in the penitent's garb, groaning and bewailing some sinful deed. For lesser sins those whose conscience was truly awakened would frequently seek counsel and advice how to plead with God for pardon, and as to the best course for them to adopt in future, so as to ease their own anxiety and to avoid such sins afterwards.

CHAPTER IV.

Confession to God followed by penance for gross sins and by daily prayer for lesser sins.

S. AUGUSTINE shows that penitence, and confession as a part of penitence, was not exacted for venial sins, he says, [1]"those whom ye see in a state of penitence have been guilty of adultery or some other enormity, for which they are put under it; if their sin had been venial, daily prayer would have been sufficient to atone for it."

S. Augustine does not at all imply any necessity for confession to any man; and thus expresses himself, [2]"What have I to do with men, that they should hear my confessions, as if they would cure me of all my distresses?"

[1] S. Augustine, Vol. VI. p. 636 de Symb. ad Catech. (Migne, Paris 1845): Illi enim quos videtis agere pœnitentiam, scelera commiserunt aut adulteria aut aliqua facta immania: inde agunt pœnitentiam. Nam si levia peccata ipsorum essent, ad hæc quotidiana oratio delenda sufficeret.

[2] S. Augustine de Confess. bk. X. ch. 3: Quid mihi ergo est cum hominibus, ut audiant confessiones meas, quasi ipsi sanaturi sint omnes languores meos.

Bellarmine quotes a passage[1] from S. Augustine's writings as an authority for enforcing the confession of all sins to the priest. The passage runs as follows: "Be downcast before thou hast confessed, having confessed, exult; now shalt thou be healed. While thou confessedst not, thy conscience collected foul matter, the abscess swelled, distressed thee, gave thee no rest; the physician foments it with words, sometimes cuts it, employs the healing knife, rebuking by tribulation. Acknowledge thou the hand of the physician; confess; let all the foul matter go forth in confession; now consult, now rejoice, what remains will readily be healed." But S. Augustine is commenting on the text "sing unto the Lord, all the whole earth," and the confession which he advocates can be confession to God only, seeing that the physician who heals by tribulation can be none other than God.

S. Augustine[2] speaks of daily prayer as the sponge

---

[1] Bellarmine de Pæn. lib. III. cap. 9: Idem (sanctus Augustinus) tractatu super Psalm. 66 docet peccata omnia esse confitenda; "Tristis esto" inquit "antequam confitearis, confessus exulta; jam sanaberis. Non confitentis conscientia saniem collegerat, apostema tumuerat, cruciabat te, requiescere non sinebat: adhibet medicus fomenta verborum et aliquando secat, adhibet medicinale ferrum in correptione tribulationis. Tu agnosce medici manum, confitere, exeat in confessione, et defluat omnis sanies, jam exulta, jam lætare, quod reliquum est facile sanabitur." Certe omnis sanies omnia peccata significat, et sicut ex apostemate omnis sanies quam diligentissime exprimenda est, ita, judice Augustino, omnia peccata in confessione aperienda sunt.

[2] S. Augustine, Sermon 181 on Sin, ch. 6: 'Dimitte nobis debita nostra.' Debita se habere confitetur quæ relaxentur. Qui non confitentur, non ideo non habent sed ideo eis non relaxabuntur. Confessio nos sanat, et vita cauta, vita humilis, oratio cum fide, contritio cordis, lacrymæ non fictæ de vena cordis profluentes, ut dimittantur nobis peccata, sine quibus esse non possumus....Talia (homicidia, adulteria,

which is to wipe away sins of infirmity, and contrasts
them with death-bringing sins, for which alone penitence is performed; and in another place he speaks[1] again
of the "three methods of remitting sins in the Church,
in baptism, in the Lord's Prayer, in the humility of the
greater penitence"; and he limits penance, and consequently confession, to sins which deserve excommunication. And in many similar passages he is a witness
that up to his time, no confession was required of any
sins, but such as subjected a man to penitential
discipline.

S. Augustine gives no counsel to confessors, how
to perform their functions. And he does not seem to
have spent his own last hours in making confession to
any other but God. He was wont to say that even
proved Christians, whether clergy or laity, should not
depart from life without a full and fitting penitence, and
this he carried out in his last illness. For he had the
Penitential Psalms copied out and arranged against the
wall in sets of four, and read them as he lay in bed
all through his sickness, and freely and bitterly wept;
and he begged that he might not be interrupted and

cætera mortifera peccata) non facit bonæ fidei et bonæ spei Christianus:
sed illa sola, quæ quotidiano orationis penicillo tergantur.

[1] S. Augustine, de Symb. ad Catech., Migne XL. p. 636: Propter
omnia peccata Baptismus inventus est; propter levia, sine quibus esse
non possumus, oratio inventa. Quid habet oratio? "Dimitte nobis
debita nostra, sicut et nos dimittimus debitoribus nostris" semel
abluimur Baptismate; quotidie abluimur oratione. Sed nolite illa
committere, pro quibus necesse est ut a Christi corpore separemini:
quod absit a nobis. Illi enim quos videtis agere pœnitentiam scelera
commiserunt aut adulteria aut aliqua facta immania: inde agunt
pœnitentiam. Nam si levia peccata ipsorum essent, ad hæc quotidiana
oratio delenda sufficeret.

that his close companions would not go into his room, except when his physicians came or he needed food, and all that time they neither read nor spoke to him.

S. Augustine exhorts those who have corrupted themselves with the *sin of incontinency* in these words[1]: "You who have so offended come in and perform your penance in the face of the Church, that you may have the benefit of its prayers. And let no man pretend to excuse himself by saying 'I repent before God, I perform it secretly within my own heart, God will pardon me, as knowing my sincerity.' For at this rate the keys would in vain be given to the Church: and the powers of binding and loosing would signify nothing. And shall we thus go about to defeat the Gospel, and to evacuate the words of Christ, our Saviour? or shall we cheat you with a promise of granting what He hath denied you?" Thus S. Augustine considered an ordinance of the Gospel defeated by what was directed by Leo, the Pope, within a few years of S. Augustine's death. He regarded the prayers of the Church to be necessary for the pardon of the sinner, but Leo determined that those of the Priest without them would be quite as effectual. Leo thought it well entirely to put an end to public confession before

---

[1] S. Augustine in Hom. XLIX. c. 3, quoted by Peter Lombard, Sent. bk. IV. dist. 17: Qui post uxores vestras vos illicito concubitu maculastis, si præter uxores vestras cum aliqua concubuistis, Agite pœnitentiam, qualis agitur in Ecclesia, ut oret pro vobis Ecclesia. Nemo sibi dicat, Occulte ago, apud Deum ago, novit Deus qui mihi ignoscat, quia in corde meo ago. Ergo sine causa dictum est, Quæ solveritis in terra soluta erunt in Cælo? Ergo sine causa sunt claves datæ Ecclesiæ Dei? Frustramus Evangelium? Frustramus verba Christi? Promittimus vobis quod ille negat?

the Church, and commanded that confession should be made to the Priest in private, whose prayers on behalf of the penitent would obtain his pardon without those of the congregation which heretofore were added.

S. Augustine's opinion[1] was that no one has true repentance, who is deterred from penance by fear of humiliation. And public penance inferred in general public confession: confession to priest or bishop had no recognized place in the African Church.

It was the practice of the Ancient Church to deny all manner of Absolution to relapsing sinners, though they could look for mercy and pardon by confession to God alone.

The iniquity of men, says S. Augustine, sometimes proceeds so far, that after they have done public penance, after they have been reconciled to the altar, they commit the same or greater sins; and yet God makes His sun to rise upon every such, and bestows upon them no less than before the greatest gifts of Life and Salvation. And [2]"though there be no place allowed to such in the Church to perform that humble sort of penance *again*, yet God does not forget His patience toward them."

In the Latin Church of the early part of the 5th

---

[1] S. Augustine on Ps. xxxiii. § 11 : Sed dicit aliquis, Quomodo ad eum accedo? Tantis malis, tantis peccatis oneratus sum, tanta scelera clamant de conscientia mea, quomodo audeo accedere ad Deum? Quomodo? Si humiliaveris te per pœnitentiam. Sed erubesco, ais, pœnitentiam agere. Accede ergo ad eum, et illuminaberis, et vultus tuus non erubescet. Si enim timor erubescendi revocat te a pœnitentia, pœnitentia autem facit te accedere ad Deum.

[2] S. Augustine, Ep. 54 ad Macedon quoted by Bingham, bk. XVIII. ch. III. § 3: Quamvis eis in Ecclesia locus humillimæ pœnitentiæ non concedatur, Deus tamen super eos suæ patientiæ non obliviscitur.

century, John Cassianus[1] states or seems to know only
public confession to God, when he counsels the sinner
who is ashamed to reveal his lapses before men, to have
recourse to the Lord, from whom nothing is hidden.
Confession to the Priest as an alternative seems to be
unknown to him.   In his monastic institutes Cassianus
orders the young monk to reveal to some older one all
the evil thoughts that arise in his mind and take counsel
with him how to avoid the snares of the enemy, but
this has nothing to do with sacramental confession, and
is akin to the monastic custom of daily confession of faults
in the chapter.

A.D. 430   S. Hilary of Arles[2] was accustomed during Lent to
preach for four hours at a time and excite the fears of
his hearers by his powerful descriptions of the torments
of Hell and the terrors of the Day of Judgment, that
the people would beg for pardon with tears and great
groanings, when he would bestow on them the imposition
of hands and pray earnestly that their repentance might
bear the proper fruit.   Here there could be no confession
except the general one of being in sin, but S. Hilary
relied upon the impression produced on the souls of the
penitents to win pardon from God.

About this time a method, by which the humiliation
of public confession was evaded, was adopted—by writing
out the confession of the penitent, which was then read
before the congregation, thus sparing him the personal
mortification of uttering it himself and of declaring himself
a sinner in the face of his companions.

[1] S. Cassian, Collat. xx. cap. 8 : Quod si verecundia retrahente,
revelare ea coram hominibus erubescis, illi quem latere non possunt,
confiteri ea jugi supplicatione non desinas.

[2] Dr Lea, Vol. I. p. 182.

* Vit. S. Hilarii Arelatens. cap. 13.

CHAPTER V.

Sins confessed to the Priest not to be published in the Church.

LEO was the first Bishop of the Latin Church who A.D. 459 by express authority made a break in the Penitential Discipline. It appears that private sins[1] after secret confession were sometimes publicly declared and read out of a Libel in the congregation and that all Bishops did not approve of this practice : therefore when Pope Leo understood that several Bishops in the provinces of

---

[1] Quoted by Bingham, bk. VIII. ch. III. § 4. Hooker, bk. VI. p. 33. Note M on Tertullian, p. 390. Marshall's Pen. Disc. p. 104. Leo, Epist. ad Episcop. Campaniæ (Migne, Paris, 1846): Ne de singulorum peccatorum genere, libello scripta professio publice recitetur; cum reatus conscientiarum sufficiat solis sacerdotibus indicari confessione secreta. Quamvis enim plenitudo fidei videatur esse laudabilis, quæ propter Dei timorem apud homines erubescere non veretur, tamen quia non omnium hujusmodi sunt peccata ut ea qui pœnitentiam poscunt, non timeant publicare removeatur tam improbabilis consuetudo, ne multi a pœnitentiæ remediis arceantur, dum aut erubescunt aut metuunt inimicis suis sua facta reserari, quibus possint legum constitutione percelli. Sufficit enim illa confessio quæ primum Deo offertur, tunc etiam sacerdoti, qui pro delictis pœnitentium precator accedit. Tunc enim demum plures ad pœnitentiam poterunt provocari si populi auribus non publicetur conscientia confitentis.

Campania, Samnium and Picenum took this method, he wrote a sharp letter to them, complaining of it as an unlawful usurpation and irregular practice to put those, who made secret confession to the Priests, upon a public rehearsal of their crimes in the face of the congregation. Which custom ought by all means to be abrogated and laid aside. Leo in his letter even commands a neglect of public humiliation. He directs them to discontinue the usage which then apparently obtained of publishing out of a writing the nature of such crimes as had been privately confessed, and that, because private confession to the Priest was, in his opinion, sufficient to the expiation of guilt. For although the fulness of their faith may seem praiseworthy which, on account of the fear of God, fears not to blush with shame before men, yet because the sins of all are not of this kind that they, who ask for penance, fear not their being published, let so unapproved a custom be removed; lest many be kept from the remedies of penance, whilst they either blush with shame or fear that their deeds should be discovered to their enemies, for which they may be punished by the appointment of the laws. For that confession is sufficient, which is offered at first to God, then also to the Priest, who draweth near in prayer for the sins of the penitent. For then at length more will be able to be provoked to penance, if the secrets of the conscience of him confessing be not published in the ears of the people.

[1] He thus disapproves of publishing the sins of penitents who are undergoing public penance.

And he also shows that *public* confession, either personally or by writing, was the only form yet recognized.

[1] Bishop of Salisbury's Letter to his Clergy (1898), p. 53 n.

In the early ages, public confession was only remitted
in the case of danger to the individual or scandal to the
Church ; by this constitution of Leo, secret confession
to the Priest was to take the place of open confession ;
and the Priest's intercession, the place of the intercession
of the Church.   The door thus opened for escaping from
the shame of public confession was never afterwards
closed and *secret confession gradually became the rule of the
Church*.   Leo, because some sins were unfit for publication, would not allow that any should be made known,
whereas the practice of the Ancient Church had been
that all sins in the first instance should be privately
confessed, and what were fit for publication, and were
not likely to be attended with other inconvenience than
with *shame* to the party by being published, these she
determined to have exposed in the open light : but those
which might probably be followed by further mischiefs,
either to the offender himself or to any one else, were
to be reserved in silence : and yet the guilty party
submitted to public penance, from whence, as Augustine[1]
observed, it was only known that some offence had been
committed, which merited such correction, though what
the actual offence was, remained a secret.   It is then
easy to see that when, with such an authority, it was
stated that confession to the Priest alone was sufficient,
few would make an acknowledgment of their sin in the
face of the congregation.   And if the Priest's intercession to God would serve all purposes, the prayers

---

[1] Bingham, bk. XVIII. ch. III. § 9: August. Serm. 16 de Verb.
Dom. cap. 8: In secreto debemus arguere, in secreto corripere: ne
volentes publice arguere, prodamus hominem.   Nos volumus corripere
et corrigere: Quid si inimicus quærit audire, quod puniat.

of the Church which had up to this time been regarded
as so important and effectual, would then be rendered
of little or no account. The public exhomologesis and
the prayers of the Church have to a great degree
been neglected ever since confession to the Priest alone
and his prayers alone have been judged effectual and
sufficient.

A.D. 470   Sinners do not seem to have availed themselves of
the opportunity of private confession, so that as a further
inducement[1] Pope Simplicius, A.D. 468—483, set apart a
week in each of the three Churches, S. Peter's, S. Paul's,
and S. Laurence's, in which priests should remain and be
prepared to receive penitents and to administer baptism
—the first authentic evidence we have of confessors
stationed in Churches,—this provision in Rome itself
shows how rare as yet was confession.

We learn from Sozomen[2] some particulars as to the

[1] Anastasius Biblioth. in Simplicio: Quare epocha hebdomadariæ
illius partitionis referri tuto potest ad pontificatum Simplicii in tribus
basilicis tunc extramænianis, intelligitur quoque apte ordinata singulis
attributis ex iis regionibus, quæ proximiores cum essent illi patriarchiali
cui ascribebantur, faciliorem obeundi ministerii copiam præbebant.

[2] Sozomen, lib. VII. ch. XVI. (Henr. Valesius, latine vertit. Paris,
MDCLXVIII): Illic enim in propatulo est pœnitentium locus: in quo
illi stant mæsti, ac veluti lugentes. Peractisque jam missarum solemni-
bus, exclusi a communione sacrorum quæ initiatis præberi mos est, cum
gemitu ac lamentis pronos se in terram abjiciunt. Tum Episcopus cum
lacrymis ex adverso occurrens, pariter ipse humi provolvitur: et
universa Ecclesiæ multitudo simul confitens, lacrymis perfunditur.
Posthæc vero primus exsurgit Episcopus, ac prostratos erigit: factaque
ut decet precatione pro peccatoribus pœnitentiam agentibus, eos
dimittit, etc.

'Ενθάδε γὰρ ἔκδηλός ἐστιν ὁ τόπος τῶν ἐν μετανοίᾳ ὄντων· ἐστᾶσι δὲ
κατηφεῖς, καὶ οἱονεὶ πενθοῦντες· ἤδη δὲ πληρωθείσης τῆς τοῦ Θεοῦ λει-
τουργίας, μὴ μετασχόντες ὧν μύσταις θέμις, σὺν οἰμωγῇ καὶ ὀδυρμῷ πρηνεῖς

way in which public penance was carried out. He tells us that "in the public penance a public station is appointed for penitents, where they stand under great appearance of lamentation and sorrow, and when so much of the Liturgy is finished as to the dismission of the Catechumens, without partaking of the Holy Mysteries with the Faithful, they, the Penitents, prostrate themselves with sighs and groans upon the ground; the Bishop meets them in this posture with tears and prostrates himself with them; the whole congregation joins with them in their mourning: then the Bishop first rises and raises those who as yet are prostrate and after putting up proper prayers to God for penitent sinners, he dismisses them. But then every man of them for himself in private mortifies himself with all manner of austerities, as he is directed by the Bishop, whose appointments he punctually observes and waits contentedly the time which is thus allotted him for his continuance under the fore-mentioned rigours: then when the period assigned him is finished and the debt, as it were, is cancelled, his sin is remitted, and he associates as before with the rest of the faithful.

ἐπὶ γῆς ῥίπτουσι σφᾶς. Ἀντιπρόσωπος δὲ δεδακρυμένος ὁ ἐπίσκοπος προσδραμών, ὁμοίως ἐπὶ τοῦ ἐδάφους πίπτει· σὺν ὀλολυγῇ καὶ τὸ πᾶν τῆς ἐκκλησίας πλῆθος δακρύων ἐμπιπλᾶται. Τὸ μετὰ τοῦτο δὲ, πρῶτος ὁ ἐπίσκοπος ἐξανίσταται, καὶ τοὺς κειμένους ἀνίστησι· καὶ ᾗ προσῆκεν ὑπὲρ ἡμαρτηκότων μεταμελουμένων εὐξάμενος, ἀποπέμπει. Καθ' ἑαυτὸν δὲ ἑκοντὶ ταλαιπωρούμενος ἕκαστος, ἢ νηστείαις, ἢ ἀλουσίαις, ἢ ἐδεσμάτων ἀποχῇ, ἢ ἑτέροις οἷς προστέτακται, περιμένει τὸν χρόνον, εἰς ὅσον αὐτῷ τέταχεν ὁ ἐπίσκοπος· τῇ δὲ προθεσμίᾳ, ὥσπερ τι ὄφλημα διαλύσας τὴν τιμωρίαν, τῆς ἁμαρτίας ἀνίεται, καὶ μετὰ τοῦ λαοῦ ἐκκλησιάζει.

εἰς ἔτι νῦν τοῦτο κρατεῖ· ἐπιμελῶς δὲ καὶ ἐν ταῖς κατὰ δύσιν ἐκκλησίαις φυλάττεται, καὶ μάλιστα ἐν τῇ Ῥωμαίων.

"This has been the usage of the *Roman Church* from the very beginning to our present age, i.e. the end of the 5th century."

The clergy and people who had heard the penitent's confession, at times prevailed upon the Bishop to allot a less remote station and a less period of humiliation.

The public confession was addressed not merely to the Bishop or the Priest in the presence of the congregation, but in a loud voice to the congregation at large. The Bishop addressed the congregation on the nature of the offence and they offered up their prayers for the offender's repentance. Such a confession signified that as the Church had been scandalised by an open sin in one of its members, reparation should be made to it by an equally open admission of sin. It also showed a reality in the offender's repentance, that he was willing to undergo this public humiliation. Doubtless the chief object was that the offender might seek the prayers of the congregation, to urge him to make a full and complete confession of his great sin, which was not only an offence to God, but was also a discredit to the Church.

But in the *Church of Constantinople*[1] there was, as

---

[1] Socrates, Hist. Eccles. lib. v. cap. 19 (and Sozomen, bk. VII. c. 16, see p. 59): Ὑπὸ δὲ τὸν αὐτὸν χρόνον, ἔδοξε καὶ τοὺς ἐπὶ τῆς μετανοίας περιελεῖν πρεσβυτέρους τῶν Ἐκκλησιῶν, δι' αἰτίαν τοιαύτην. Ἀφ' οὗ Ναυατιανοὶ τῆς Ἐκκλησίας διεκρίθησαν, τοῖς ἐπταικόσιν ἐν τῷ ἐπὶ Δεκίου διωγμῷ κοινωνῆσαι μὴ θελήσαντες, οἱ ἐπίσκοποι τῷ ἐκκλησιαστικῷ κανόνι τὸν πρεσβύτερον τὸν ἐπὶ τῆς μετανοίας προσέθεσαν, ὅπως ἂν οἱ μετὰ τὸ βάπτισμα πταίσαντες, ἐπὶ τοῦ προβληθέντος τούτου πρεσβυτέρου ἐξομολογῶνται τὰ ἁμαρτήματα. Οὗτος ὁ κανὼν κρατεῖ μέχρι νῦν ἐν ταῖς ἄλλαις αἱρέσεσι....ἐπὶ Νεκταρίου τοῦ ἐπισκόπου μετέθεσαν, τοιούτου τινὸς ἐπὶ τὴν ἐκκλησίαν συμβάντος. Γυνή τις τῶν εὐγενῶν προσῆλθεν τῷ ἐπὶ τῆς μετανοίας πρεσβυτέρῳ· καὶ κατὰ μέρος ἐξομολογεῖται τὰς ἁμαρτίας, ἃς

we have stated above, a distinct presbyter appointed to take care of penitents, until such a scandal arose that Nectarius abolished the office of Penitentiary Presbyter, which constitution of his has remained in force from that time to the present. Nectarius admitted all to communicate as their own consciences should direct or embolden them, and if they partook unworthily they were to answer for it to God and their own consciences.

This seems to imply that it had been the custom for the people to consult with the Penitentiary, when they felt the guilt of some sin, before presenting themselves to receive the Eucharist; and that after the office of the Penitentiary was abolished, people only consulted their own consciences.

In the 6th century, the practice of making confession of *public* sins to the Bishop, and of *private* ones to the Priest, arose. And when the office of Penitentiary was abolished by the Bishop of Constantinople the confession of *secret* sins to God only became the avowed practice of the *Greek* Church.

It appears however that public penance for sins was undergone, even when no public confession of the sin was made before the congregation. All that was generally

ἐπεπράχει μετὰ τὸ βάπτισμα. Ὁ δὲ πρεσβύτερος παρήγγειλε τῇ γυναικί, νηστεύειν καὶ συνεχῶς εὔχεσθαι ἵνα σὺν τῇ ὁμολογίᾳ καὶ ἔργον τι δεικνύειν ἔχῃ τῆς μετανοίας ἄξιον. Ἡ δὲ γυνὴ προβαίνουσα, καὶ ἄλλο πταῖσμα ἑαυτῆς κατηγόρει. Ἔλεγε γὰρ, ὡς εἴη συγκαθευδήσας αὐτῇ τῆς ἐκκλησίας διάκονος. Τοῦτο λεχθὲν, τὸν μὲν διάκονον τῆς Ἐκκλησίας ἐκπεσεῖν παρεσκεύασε. Ταραχὴ δὲ κατέσχε τὰ πλήθη· ἠγανάκτουν γὰρ οὐ μόνον ἐπὶ τῷ γενομένῳ, ἀλλ' ὅτι καὶ τῇ Ἐκκλησίᾳ βλασφημίαν ἡ πρᾶξις καὶ ὕβριν προὐξένησεν. Διασυρομένων δὲ ἐκ τούτου τῶν ἱερωμένων ἀνδρῶν, Εὐδαίμων τις τῆς Ἐκκλησίας πρεσβύτερος, Ἀλεξανδρεὺς τὸ γένος γνώμην τῷ ἐπισκόπῳ δίδωσι Νεκταρίῳ, περιελεῖν μὲν τὸν ἐπὶ τῆς μετανοίας πρεσβύτερον· συγχωρήσει δὲ ἕκαστον, τῷ ἰδίῳ συνειδότι τῶν μυστηρίων μετέχειν.

known[1] was that those, whom they saw performing acts of penance in the Church, were guilty of some great sin.

A.D. 529   In the Rule of Benedict[2], private confession is not imposed upon the inmates of the monastery, but is recommended as a sign of humility, and a monk, who is conscious that there is lurking within him a thought or desire which might lead him into sin, is bid to reveal it to the Abbot or to one of the elders, who know how to cure wounds and not betray them. As the Abbots of the period were seldom priests, there was nothing sacramental about these regulations.

The necessity of confession to a priest or bishop was not in the middle of the 6th century impressed on the mind of Victor[3] of Tunnone, for he seems to regard confession to God as the one thing needful to produce true repentance and to obtain pardon for sin. The very act of confession to God, in his opinion, cures the soul. Man in his time still directly dealt with God, and required no intermediary.

[1] S. Augustine, Vol. VI. p. 636, de Symb. ad Catech. (Migne, Paris, 1845), see p. 65.

[2] Dr Lea, Auricular Confession, Vol. I. p. 184.

* Reg. S. Benedicti, cap. VII. 45, 46.

[3] Dr Lea, Vol. I. p. 181.

* Victor Tunenens. de Pœn. lib. I. cap. 3.

CHAPTER VI.

Penitentials.

IT appears that towards the end of the 6th century A.D. 580
it was found desirable to establish a systematic form of
procedure for ' penance ' and to appoint a definite period
for the penitent to remain under penance according to
the nature of the sin committed. These books of
directions were termed[1] ' Penitentials.' From the Greek
Penitentials we learn that confession was made sitting :
the penitent kneeling only twice while making his
confession—at the beginning, when the Priest asked the

---

[1] Lingard, Anglo-Saxon Church, I. 334 : By the word 'Penitential'
was understood a set of regulations made for the guidance of Confessors,
that in the imposition of penance they might act according to the spirit
of the ancient canons, when they could no longer enforce them according to the letter. With this view compilations had been made and
preserved in the different Churches, but they were all subsequently
thrown into the shade by the penitential which Archbishop Theodore
composed for the use of the English Church. His authority was
sufficient to ensure its adoption among the Bishops of his province:
its merit or reputation led to its introduction into the neighbouring
Churches on the Continent, where it long formed the ground-work of
the penitential codes followed in most dioceses. The principal species
of punishment was fasting.

Holy Spirit's aid to move the man to unburden his soul completely as to the details and motives of his sin, and at the end, when a prayer was offered up that he might obtain grace to perform his sentence conscientiously. The origin of this custom was due to the great length to which the form and process of confessing extended. The practice has since continued in the Greek Church for both priest and penitent to sit.

In the Penitential of Johannes Jejunator, who was raised to the See of Constantinople, A.D. 585, we learn the mode in which confessions were then received. "He who comes to confess ought to make three inclinations of the body as he approaches the sacred Altar and say three times 'I confess to thee, O God, Lord God of heaven and earth, whatever is in the secret places of my heart,' and after he has so done he should raise himself and stand erect, and he who receives his confession should question him with a cheerful and gentle voice......" and then follow 95 questions, and the Priest orders the penitent, if not a woman, to uncover his head, even though he wear a crown; he then prays with him; after that he raises him and bids him recover his head and sits with him and asks him what penance he can bear.

During the period people were undergoing their time of penance, the men had their heads shaven, and the women were veiled; their garments were of sackcloth, sprinkled with ashes, and they were required to abstain from wine and meat. The filthier the penitent the more beautiful.

The following prayers[1] and details at receiving penitents to penance and at hearing their confession are

[1] Marshall's Pen. Disc. Appendix, p. 204.

translated from the Greek and taken out of the Penitential of Johannes Jejunator, and from that of Theodore, Archbishop of Canterbury.

The penitent was placed[1] before the Altar and the Penitential service began with chanting certain Psalms (vi., xxiv., l., xxxi., lxix., ci.), then some few formularies were used and the Priest offered up a prayer before receiving the confession of the Penitent. "O Lord God, the Father and Lord of all men, who beholdest all things and dost indulgently extend thy pardon to such as turn unto thee from their sinful ways......Who wouldest have all to be saved and come to the knowledge of thy Truth, who dost rejoice at the repentance of a sinner and desiredst not his death, but wouldest rather that he should be converted and live ; do thou, O most merciful Saviour, hearken, I beseech thee, to my intercession...... Hear me therefore, O Lord, according to the multitude of thy mercies, though I have sinned against thee, and receive the confession of thy servant, who is now before thee, and whatsoever guilt he may have contracted either through frailty or through wilfulness, by thought, word, or deed, do thou, I beseech thee, in much mercy forgive it, for thou only canst do it ; and therefore before thee we prostrate ourselves in fervent prayer, and do glorify thy holy name, to whom with the Father and the Holy Ghost, be all praise and honour, now and ever."

It appears that Penitential Books were of Eastern origin and that that of John, Patriarch of Constantinople,

---

[1] Penitential of Johannes Jejunator (Morini Tract. de Pœnit.): Assumit Sacerdos peccata confessurum et sistit eum coram altari, cantatque cum eo trisagion, et Psalmum sextum, Domine ne in furore tuo arguas me, et Psalmum 24, Ad te Domine levavi animam meam, &c.

was the earliest of them and was founded on a previous collection of Canons of Stephanus Epiphanius. This John was in strong antagonism with Gregory the Great. The first Penitential[1] in the Western Church dates about 100 years afterwards and was drawn up A.D. 680 by Theodore, the Greek Archbishop of Canterbury. In the Penitential of John of Constantinople there is the precise direction[2] "that bishops, priests and deacons are

---

[1] Thorpe, 277 seq., Ancient Laws and Institutes of England, fol. Edit. Liber Pœnitentialis Theodori Archiepiscopi Cantuariensis Ecclesiæ.

Qualiter apud Orientales provincias Germaniæ atque Saxoniæ pro diversis criminibus, pœnitentiæ observatur modus.

Si quis, pro qualicunque criminali peccato, diutina pœnitentia fuerit puniendus, placuit quibusdam, ut tam diu ab ingressu æcclesiæ amoveatur, quam diu pœnitentiæ ipsius mensura extenditur. Nonnullis etiam in locis ita observatur, ut si quis VII annorum vel VII carinarum pœnitentia fuerit damnatus, primo anno vel prima carina se ab introitu æcclesiæ abstineat: deinde semper tres quadragesimas per sex sequentes annos custodiat......Quosdam etiam vidimus, quibus, per omnes VII annos, commorandi uno loco, nisi unius diei et noctis (spatio), interdicta erat licentia, excepta infirmitatis causa vel causa præcipuæ festivitatis.

This is followed by 49 sections, giving details of the penance for various sins, of the reconciliation of penitents, of women in Church— and of the pollution of a Church in which 'unfaithful' persons have been buried: both Theodore and Ecgbert say "it is lawful for women to receive the Eucharist under a black veil, as Basil commanded."

[2] Joh. Jejunator, Libellus Pœnitentialis, Morini Tract. de Pœnit. Append. pp. 85, 86: Sacerdotes enim et Episcopi et Diaconi, qui in gradu sunt vel eorum uxores, ad peccatorum confessionem suscipiendi non sunt, nisi secundum Deum securitatem eorum confessoribus fecerint, quod si alicujus criminis rei sunt quod eos a sacris ordinibus exercendis prohibeat, non amplius sacris ministrare audebunt. Ejusmodi enim non datur Pœnitentia, qualiscunque illa sit, sive cibi, sive potus nequidem omnino a communione abstinentia; sed sola a sacro ministerio cessatio.

not to be heard in confession, unless they furnish security
in advance that if they have done aught which should
prevent performance of their functions, they will not
minister in future; for no penance can be assigned to
them. They may still however officiate as lector and
need not abstain from communion.

The following is a Prayer[1] for Penitents accompanied
with imposition of hands, in constant use in public worship,
to be found in the Apostolical Constitutions and therefore
much earlier than the Penitentials :—

"Almighty and eternal God, Lord of the Universe,
Creator and Governor of all things, Who, through thy
Son, Jesus Christ, hast cleansed man, and made him the
ornament of this lower world, and hast given him a law
in his heart, as well as a written word, that he might

---

[1] Marshall's Pen. Disc. Appendix, No. IV. p. 202. Constit.
Apostol. bk. VIII. ch. IX. Cotelerius: Παντοκράτορ θεὲ αἰώνιε, δέσποτα
τῶν ὅλων, κτίστα καὶ πρύτανι τῶν πάντων· ὁ τὸν ἄνθρωπον κόσμου κόσμον
ἀναδείξας διὰ Χριστοῦ, καὶ νόμον δοὺς αὐτῷ ἔμφυτον καὶ γραπτὸν, πρὸς
τὸ ζῆν αὐτὸν ἐνθέσμως, ὡς λογικόν· καὶ ἁμαρτόντι ὑποθήκην δοὺς πρὸς
μετάνοιαν τὴν σαυτοῦ ἀγαθότητα· ἔπιδε ἐπὶ τοὺς κεκλικόσας σοι αὐχένα,
ψυχῆς καὶ σώματος· ὅτι οὐ βούλει τὸν θάνατον τοῦ ἁμαρτωλοῦ, ἀλλὰ τὴν
μετάνοιαν, ὥστε ἀποστρέψαι αὐτὸν ἀπὸ τῆς ὁδοῦ αὐτοῦ τῆς πονηρᾶς, καὶ
ζῆν. ὁ Νινευϊτῶν προσδεξάμενος τὴν μετάνοιαν· ὁ θέλων πάντας ἀνθρώ-
πους σωθῆναι, καὶ εἰς ἐπίγνωσιν ἀληθείας ἐλθεῖν· ὁ τὸν υἱὸν προσδεξάμενος,
τὸν καταφαγόντα τὸν βίον αὐτοῦ ἀσώτως, πατρικοῖς σπλάγχνοις, διὰ τὴν
μετάνοιαν· αὐτὸς καὶ νῦν πρόσδεξαι τῶν ἱκετῶν σου τὴν μετάγνωσιν· ὅτι
οὐκ ἔστιν ὃς οὐχ ἁμαρτήσεταί σοι· ἐὰν γὰρ ἀνομίας παρατηρήσῃ, κύριε,
κύριε, τίς ὑποστήσεται; ὅτι παρὰ σοὶ ὁ ἱλασμός ἐστι· καὶ ἀποκατάστησον
αὐτοὺς τῇ ἁγίᾳ σου ἐκκλησίᾳ, ἐν τῇ προτέρᾳ ἀξίᾳ καὶ τιμῇ, διὰ τοῦ Χριστοῦ
τοῦ Θεοῦ καὶ σωτῆρος ἡμῶν· δι' οὗ σοι δόξα καὶ προσκύνησις, ἐν τῷ ἁγίῳ
πνεύματι, εἰς τοὺς αἰῶνας. ἀμήν.

καὶ ὁ διάκονος λεγέτω· ἀπολύεσθε οἱ ἐν μετανοίᾳ, καὶ προστιθέτω·
μήτις τῶν μὴ δυναμένων προελθέτω· ὅσοι πιστοί, κλίνωμεν γόνυ· δεηθῶμεν
τοῦ Θεοῦ διὰ τοῦ Χριστοῦ αὐτοῦ, πάντες συντόνως τὸν Θεὸν διὰ τοῦ Χριστοῦ
αὐτοῦ παρακαλέσωμεν.

live according to thy will, as becomes a reasonable creature, and after he had sinned didst extend thy goodness towards him to lead him to repentance; Thou, who desirest not the death of a sinner, but wouldest rather that he should turn from his evil way and live, look graciously upon these thy servants, who here bow down themselves before thee, in humiliation and repentance. Thou, who didst accept the repentance of the Ninevites, turning to thee, who wouldst have all men to be saved and come to the knowledge of thy truth, Thou, who didst receive with a fatherly compassion thy prodigal son, though he had spent all his substance in riotous living, seeing at last that he was sorry for his sin, receive in like manner, we most humbly beseech thee, the supplications of those who turn now unto thee in penitential tears, for there is none amongst us who sinneth not against thee and in thy sight, and if thou, Lord, shouldest be extreme to mark what is done amiss, O Lord, who may abide with thee? But there is mercy with thee [extend it, therefore, we earnestly beg, to these thy servants]; restore them to the bosom of thy Holy Church, and to the place and station which they before held in it, through Jesus Christ our Saviour, by whom, in the Holy Ghost, be all honour and adoration ascribed to thee, world without end. Amen."

When it was finished, the Deacon proclaimed, "Depart all you who are in the station of penance"; and added moreover, "Let none depart but those who are appointed. Let us who are in the number of the faithful pray to God through his Son, Christ."

Explicit directions[1] are given in the Penitential of

[1] Maskell's Doctrine of Absolution, pp. 100, 101. Morinus, De

Archbishop Ecgbert, as to the manner of receiving the confession of a penitent by the Priest. This would be about the year A.D. 770. The Priest is to offer up certain prayers to God on behalf of the penitent to the intent that God will give him perfect knowledge and true understanding to confess truly his sins. Then the priest is directed to say several psalms with three other prayers for the penitent: after which he is to examine him as to the Articles of the Creed and whether he knows the Lord's Prayer. After this he is to question him as to his sins. "Tell me the works which you have done or thought of." Then follow some forms of Confession intended to lead the penitent to confess fully his sins: ending thus, "May all things be done in pure confession to the Lord God Almighty and to thee, the friend and priest of God, and I ask thee with all humility to pray that He will of his mercy grant me pardon of my sins." The priest then says, "May Almighty God, who has said, whosoever confesses me before men, him will I also confess before my Father, bless thee and give thee remission of sins." Other prayers, collects and psalms are then to be said, and then the benediction is pronounced over the penitent. "May Almighty God have mercy on thee, and forgive thee all thy sins, may He deliver thee from all evil, keep thee in every good thing and lead thee to everlasting life."

pœnit., Antiqui Pœnitentiales, p. 13: "Confessio peccatorum." Quando volueris confessionem facere peccatorum tuorum, viriliter age et confortare in Domino et noli erubescere: et quia inde venit indulgentia, cum in spe misericordiæ Dei humiliter confessus fueris peccata tua, et reliqueris ea, quia sine confessione non est indulgentia.

Then follow various forms of Confession, and details of the whole course of penitents.

The Greek Penitentials of the end of the 6th century, and the Latin ones of a century later, give no hint of habitual confession of common infirmities but refer to definite sins of a gross character, neither is there in these Penitentials any intimation of private confession being a matter of indispensable obligation, still less of the doctrine that one may daily confess and be daily and plenarily absolved. In A.D. 680 the first Penitential Book in the Western Church appeared. It was drawn up, as stated above, by Theodore of Canterbury. This soon gained a great authority in the continental churches, as well as in England. The object of Theodore was to reduce penance to something practicable, as the impossibility of fulfilling the requirements of the ancient canons had led to a general evasion or disregard of them.

A.D. 600   He gives, however, a rule which shows that auricular confession was not yet obligatory, when he states that "confession, if needful, may be made to God only." The Penitentials which were issued after this contain some indication of the treatment of penitents by confessors, but these show how rare confession was as yet.

CHAPTER VII.

Public Confession and public Penance seldom practised.

GREGORY the Great[1], whose Pontificate extended from A.D. 580 to 604, did much to advance sacerdotalism,

[1] Gregory, Hom. in Evang. bk. II. Hom. 26: Veniat itaque foras mortuus, id est culpam confiteatur peccator. Venientem vero foras solvant discipuli, ut pastores Ecclesiæ ei pœnam debeant amovere quam meruit, qui non erubuit confiteri quod fecit.

Gregory, Moral. Lib. VIII. cap. 21: Sciendum quoque est quia sæpe et reprobi peccata confitentur, sed deflere contemnunt. Electi autem culpas suas, quas vocibus confessionis aperiunt, districtæ animadversionis fletibus insequuntur.

Gregory, Moral. Lib. XXV. cap. 13: Nam sicut in vulnere ab internis trahitur virus in cute, ita in confessione peccati, dum in publicum secreta panduntur, quasi mali humores a visceribus intimis foras prorumpunt.

Gregory, Lib. VI. Expos. in 1 Reg. c. 15: Catervatim nunc in flagitia corruunt non solum subjecti debiles, sed etiam Prælati et sacerdotes negligentes: sed plerique eorum, dum quodammodo ad cor redeunt, se errasse confitentur; qui tamen sic volunt contra se peccata proferre, ut velint adhuc de officio sacri Ordinis honorari. Turpes in secreto se proferunt, sed foris præter Ordinis celsitudinem videri humiles erubescunt.

Signum ergo veræ confessionis non est in oris confessione, sed in afflictione pœnitentiæ. Tunc namque bene conversum peccatorem cernimus, cum digna afflictionis austeritate delere nititur, quod loquendo confitetur.

and takes it that it is a matter of course that confession is necessary for the remission of sins, and that the process is in the hands of priests. He speaks of the *public* confession of *secret* sins, not only as a healthy exercise but also as a practice still followed, but he admits that it was difficult after private confession to bring men to submit to public discipline. He tells us of the looseness which generally then prevailed amongst all orders and degrees of men: how "both Priests and people run riot in wickedness, and when they were any way prevailed upon to come to themselves, so far as to confess their faults, yet would they not submit to be censured for them, nor to appear in a posture becoming penitents," from which it appears that he was desirous to revive the ancient relation between private confession and public penance.

"[1] We learn from the answer given by S. Gregory to Augustine that although it differed from the Roman, yet in his judgment the Gallican or (if we may so conclude it) the British Liturgy contained nothing that was objectionable." And Maskell also (p. 15) tells us that "in most ancient offices we find forms of confession and absolution before the more solemn part of the Liturgy: they are in the Liturgy of S. James which, next to the Clementine, is acknowledged as the oldest extant. The Gallican Liturgy contains them under another name 'Apologia.'"

After this time, the beginning of the 7th century, there seems to be no evidence of the existence of *public confession*; and after private confession, penitents seldom submitted to public penance.

---

[1] Maskell, Ancient Liturgies of the Church of England, p. lviii.

In the 7th century the stern rule[1], that solemn confession, as a part of penitence, was received only once, had become obsolete, but habitual confession had not yet taken its place. The growth however of Penitentials indicates how the practice of confession spread and how firmly it became lodged in priestly hands.

In Spain S. Isidor of Seville[2], early in the 7th century, gives a very precise account of the duties of bishop and priest but says nothing of their hearing confessions : he recognizes the public penance of sinners, appearing in sackcloth and ashes, but in no way alludes to the secret confession to the priest of the ordinary sins of frailty, of irregularities of life, or of evil motives of the natural heart, nor does he make any mention of private penance.

In the East, at the same period, S. Dorotheus the Abbot, in his instructions as to securing salvation, speaks of repentance and amendment and prayer and doing good, but makes no reference to confession or to the ministrations of the priest in connection with it.

A council of Toledo[3] decided that if a man in mortal A.D. 633

---

[1] Origen, Hom. xv. in Lev. : In gravioribus enim criminibus semel tantum, vel raro pœnitentiæ conceditur locus: ista vero communia, quæ frequenter incurrimus, semper pœnitentiam recipiunt, et sine intermissione redimuntur.

[2] S. Isidori Hispalens. de Eccl. Officiis Lib. II. cap. XVII. 4—7 : Bene ergo in cilicio et cinere pœnitens deplorat peccatum, quia in cilicio asperitas est, et punctio peccatorum, in cinere autem pulvis ostenditur mortuorum. Et idcirco in utroque pœnitentiam agimus, ut et punctione cilicii agnoscamus vitia, quæ per culpam commisimus: et per favillam cineris perpendamus mortis sententiam, ad quam peccando pervenimus......ita per pœnitentiæ compunctionem fructuosam universa fateamur deleri peccata.

[3] Dr Lea, Vol. I. p. 46.

* Concil. Toletan. IV. ann. 633, c. liv.

sickness accepted penance but only made a general confession that he was a sinner : if he recovered, he was eligible to ordination, but any one who had *publicly* confessed a mortal sin, must still be excluded.

For *public* sins a cleric was deposed from his office on account of the scandal to the Church, while for *secret* sins he could confess and perform penance.

A.D. 650   The first Council of Châlons, A.D. 650, declares (c. 8) "that all agree that confession to a priest is a proof of penitence."

At the 10th Council of Toledo[1], A.D. 656, Potamius, Archbishop of Braga, made a confession in writing, charging himself with misdemeanours. The confession had in no way been forced from him, he does not appear to have been subjected to any kind of accusation, and the Council was so taken with surprise, that at first it refused to believe his statement. But on his declaring that his confession was but too true, he was deposed from his archbishopric and subjected to penance during the remainder of his life.

The venerable Bede[2] considers that the only sins, which ought to be brought before the notice of the Church, are heresy, infidelity, Judaism and schism, and that God cleanses sinners of all other sins when His mercy is sought by prayer : He then influences the mind

---

[1] Smith's Dict. of Christ. Antiq. "exhomologesis."

[2] Bedæ in Lucæ Evang. Exposit. Lib. v. cap. 17 (Migne, Paris, 1850): Et quisquis vel hæretica pravitate, vel superstitione gentili vel Iudaica perfidia, vel etiam schismate fraterno, quasi vario colore per Domini gratiam caruerit, necesse est ad Ecclesiam veniat, coloremque fidei verum, quem acceperit, ostendat. Cetera vero vitia tanquam valetudinis, et quasi membrorum animæ atque sensuum per seipsum interius in conscientia et intellectu Dominus sanat et corrigit.

of the offender so that he abandons his former evil-doing. He draws a distinction, as in former ages, between confession of frailties and of heinous sins—thus[1], " we ought to use this discretion, our daily light sins confess to one another, and hope that by our prayers they may be healed, but the pollution of the greater leprosy, let us according to the law open to the priest, and in the manner and the time which he directs purify ourselves."

Bede, when describing the last hours of certain holy persons and mentioning that they received the Holy Communion before their death, gives no intimation that they made any kind of confession before partaking.

Morinus[2] dates the prevalence of the custom of making a distinction as to public penance between secret and open sins A.D. 700—730,—the time of Bede. 　　A.D. 700

Towards the end of the 7th century there was a notable case[3] of numbers of persons, conscience-stricken for their sin, flocking to an old hermit of the name of Guthlac, who had retired from the world and set up a poor hut of wicker-work in the swamps of East Anglia. He suffered many ills of body but continually poured forth his soul to God. To him they made confession of their sins, for he was regarded as a saint by the people. He sympathized with them and imparted to them some

[1] Bede, Exp. in S. Jacob. v.: Illa debet esse discretio ut quotidiana leviaque peccata alterutrum coæqualibus confiteamur, eorumque quotidiana credamus oratione salvari. Porro gravioris lepræ immunditiam juxta legem sacerdoti pandamus, atque ad ejus arbitrium qualiter, et quanto tempore jusserit, purificare curemus.

[2] Pamphlet of Bishop of Salisbury on the Ministry of Penance, 1898, p. 53, Note §.　* Morinus, VII. l.

[3] Wakeman, Hist. of Church of England, p. 51.

of the comfort which he had himself obtained by prayer to God.   He was a man devoted to converse with God, but no priest of the Church.   After his death the swamps were drained, and on the spot where he had passed several years in retirement from the world and in devotion to God those, who admired the manner in which he struggled against his infirmities, united with those who had gained from him some consolation after they had opened their hearts, laden with sin, to him, and these raised to his memory the famous monastery of Crowland.

CHAPTER VIII.

Periodical Confession.

THE earliest attempt at inducing periodical confession would seem to be by[1] Egbert of York in the latter half of the 8th century: who says that Theodore of Canterbury introduced the custom that within 12 days of Christmas all, both clerics and laymen, should seek their Confessors, as a preparation for the Communion of the Nativity.

In 779 Charlemagne limited the privilege of asylum A.D. 779 in Churches by enacting that murderers or other capital

---

[1] Ecberti Dialog. Interrog. XVI. : Ecclesia catholica morem obtinet, et jejunium atque observationem mense celebrat decimo, sabbato quarto, propter advenientem venerabilem solemnitatem Domini nostri, Iesu Christi: ubi ante plures dies et continentia carnis et jejunia exhibenda sunt, ut unusquisque fidelis præparet se ad communionem corporis et sanguinis Christi, cum devotione sumendam. Quod et Anglorum semper in plena hebdomada ante Natale Domini consuerit, non solum quarta et sexta feria, et sabbato, sed et juges duodecim dies in jejuniis et vigiliis et orationibus, eleemosynarum largitionibus et in monasteriis et in plebibus, ante Natale Domini, quasi legitimum jejunium exercuisse perhibetur. Nam hæc a temporibus Vitaliani papæ et Theodori Dorobernensis archiepiscopi inolevit in Ecclesia Anglorum consuetudo et quasi legitima tenebatur, ut non solum clerici in monasteriis sed etiam laici cum conjugibus et familiis suis ad confessores suos pervenirent.

offenders should not be allowed to take refuge in churches, and that if they gained admittance, no food should be given them. But the clergy soon discovered a way of evading this law by construing it as applicable to impenitent criminals only—i.e. to such as should refuse to confess to the priest, and to undergo ecclesiastical penance—a refusal[1] which would not be likely to be frequent, where it involved the choice between starvation and loss of sanctuary.

A.D. 790 About A.D. 790 Alcuin, in writing to the brethren in Aquitaine and Languedoc, praises highly their piety and reverence, but reproves them[2] because he is told that no layman is willing to confess to a priest.

In the year 793 Alcuin, writing to the monks of Tynemouth, urges them[3] to adopt private confession.

In spite of the exhortations and commands to confess annually, it is apparent from the formulas in the Penitentials and the books of ritual that voluntary confession was as yet an extraordinary incident in the life of a sinner and a somewhat unusual one in that of a priest. The long recital of sins from childhood to maturity, provided for, shows that penitents were expected to come forward only when in fear of approaching

---

[1] Robertson, Church History, Vol. II. p. 227.

* Pertz, I. 36 and Planck, II. 259, 260.

[2] Alcuini Ep. CXII.: Dicitur vero neminem ex laicis suam velle confessionem sacerdotibus dare.

[3] Alcuini Ep. XIV.: Si quid peccati pro fragilitate carnis commiserit, abluat confessione, deleat pœnitentia, ne damnetur in pœna sed coronetur in gloria. Habetis sanctos Patres qui vos genuerunt adjutores, si illorum præceptorum eritis factores......per vestras intercessiones veniam habere merear meorum delictorum, et vos mercedem fraternæ dilectionis apud Deum habeatis æternam.

death, or of some unusual danger, and that the accumu-
lated misdeeds of a lifetime were to be expressed by
words in a single effort to quiet the conscience. Then
they sought to gain some relief by taking another into
their confidence.

The long protracted ceremonies[1], moreover, of which
the details have been handed down to us, rendered it
impossible for a priest to receive the Confession of more
than a very few penitents, and could only have been
established at a time when a confession was an excep-
tional occurrence. When a penitent applies, the priest
is instructed to retire to his " cubiculum," or prayer-
cell, and pray to God, as a preliminary, after which he
returns to the sinner, preaches a sermon to him, or

---

[1] Martene, de antiq. Eccles. Ritibus, Lib. I. cap. VI. Art. 7.
Editio secunda, Antverp. 1736.

Ordo 2. Ex MSS. Pontificali Anglicano monasterii Gemmeticensis,
cujus caracter annos circiter nongentos refert.

In primis dicit psalmum XXXVII. totum : Domine, ne in furore tuo
arguas me : Et postea dicit, Oremus : Exaudi quæsumus Domine
supplicum preces, et confitentium tibi parce peccatis, ut quos con-
scientiæ reatus accusat, indulgentia tuæ miserationis absolvat Per......

Psalm CII. followed by a Prayer;

also Psalm L. and LI. followed by Prayer,

ending with one of several forms of Absolution.

Ordo 6. Ex pervetusco codice Gellonensi sæculo IX. et X.

Formæ Absolutionis pœnitentis morientis.

Ordo 12. Ex MS. Bibliothecæ Regiæ num. 3866 ab annis circiter
600 scripto.

Ordo pœnitentis ad mortem.

In primis cum pœnitens venerit ad confitendum dicat sacerdos intra
se : Domine, Deus omnipotens, qui non vis mortem peccatorum : sed
ut convertantur et vivant : propitius esto mihi peccatori et suscipe
orationem etc....Et cum confessus fuerit peccata sua dicat illi sacerdos
quod non desperet de venia vel de misericordia Dei, sed firmiter teneat
quia salvus erit, si ipsa hora mortuus fuerit etc.

perhaps even says mass over him, and at the least sings several psalms, listens to the circumstances and particulars of the sins committed, consults with the penitent as to the amount of penance that he can endure, determines of what kind and of what duration the penance shall be, and concludes with a number of prayers. Still more convincing, as to the rarity of such confession being made, is the fact that in many of the "Ordines" the priest is directed to encourage the penitent by sharing with him a portion of the penance and fasting with him for two or three weeks—an amount of self-sacrifice only to be expected when penitents were very few in number, and scarcely adapted to lead the priest to encourage confession among his flock unless some notable pecuniary advantage was anticipated as a result.

A.D. 813   We learn from the Second Council of Châlons, A.D. 813, that secret confession was not yet a matter of obligation[1]. "Some say they ought to confess their sins to God only, and some think they are to be confessed unto the priests, both of which, not without great fruit, are practised in the Holy Church; the confession which is made to God

---

[1] Canon of the Second Council of Châlons, c. 33: Quidam Deo solummodo confiteri debere dicunt peccata, quidam vero sacerdotibus confitenda esse percensent: quod utrumque non sine magno fructu intra sanctam fit Ecclesiam. Ita dumtaxat ut et Deo, qui remissor est peccatorum, confiteamur peccata nostra, et cum David dicamus "Delictum meum cognitum tibi feci, et injustitiam meam non abscondi; dixi confitebor adversum me injustitias meas domino, et tu remisisti impietatem peccati mei." Et secundum institutionem apostoli, confiteamur alterutrum peccata nostra et oremus pro invicem ut salvemur. Confessio itaque, quæ Deo sit, purgat peccata: ea vero quæ sacerdoti sit, docet qualiter ipsa purgentur peccata. Deus namque salutis et sanitatis auctor et largitor, plerumque hanc præbet suæ potentiæ invisibili administratione plerumque medicorum operatione.

purgeth sins, that made to the priests teacheth in what way those sins should be purged."

And so it remained an open question for 400 years, as to any necessity to confess to a priest, until the Council of Lateran, A.D. 1215.

The same Council of Châlons gives precise directions on the manner and order of receiving the Holy Communion, but not a word about the manner of receiving people's confession, although private confession had undoubtedly taken the place of penitential confession in the 9th century.

Pilgrimage regarded as penance.

The Council, however, complains that people coming to confess neglect to do so fully, and orders each one, when he comes, to examine himself and make confession of the eight capital sins which prevail in the world, viz., drunkenness, pride, sloth, wrath, sadness, avarice, gluttony, and lust, and it may be assumed of no others. This Council acknowledges the benefit of pilgrimage[1] for those who have confessed their sins and have obtained directions for penance, who amend their lives, give alms and practise devotions, but it denounces the error of such as consider pilgrimage a licence to sin.

In some cases persons who had been guilty of grievous sin were condemned by way of penance to leave their country, and either to wander for a time or to undertake a pilgrimage to some particular place. Many of them were loaded with chains or with rings, which ate into

---

[1] Robertson, History of the Christian Church, Vol. II. p. 222.

* Martene, I. 268.

the flesh and inflicted excessive torture. Ethelwulf, the father of Alfred the Great, at his visit to Rome in the year 855, obtained from Benedict III. the privilege that no Englishman should ever be obliged to undergo this sort of penance.

A.D. 797   Theodulph's Capitulary, c. 30, draws a distinction between confession made to a priest and that to God only, and c. 31 mentions the same eight principal sins as the Council of Châlons, and appoints that every one learning to confess should be examined on what occasions and in what manner he had been guilty of any of them, and consequently to be subjected to no further examination.

He orders, c. 36, confessions to be made the week before Lent.

So little conception was there in the Church of the period of any Sacramental character attaching to private confession that Theodulph, who prescribed it annually, orders daily confession to God, and regards that to the priest only as an assistance whereby to obtain wholesome counsel as to penance and mutual prayer.

Chrodegang orders confession to be made at each of the three fasts of the year, adding " he who does more does better," and he directs the monks to confess every Saturday to the Bishop or their Prior.

Penitents no longer excluded from full Communion.

A.D. 814   At this time, A.D. 814, Confession of secret sins[1] was much insisted on, but the priest was regarded rather as an

---

[1] Robertson, History of the Christian Church, Vol. II. p. 224.

* Planck, II. 316.

adviser than as a judge, and the form of his Absolution was not judicial but in the form of a prayer to God for His mercy. Absolution was usually given immediately after confession, and the prescribed penance was left to be performed afterwards, so that, whereas in earlier ages the penitents had been excluded for a time from the full communion of the Church, they now remained in it throughout.

The power of the Pope, in the matter of Penance, creeps in.

Every Bishop had been formerly regarded as the sole judge in cases of penance within his own Diocese—as the only person who could relax the penance which he had himself imposed. The Bishop's power of Absolution was still unassailed: there was not as yet any thought of cases being reserved for the decision of the Pope alone. But the popes began to claim a jurisdiction as to penance similar to that which they were gradually establishing over the Church in other respects: they asserted a right of absolving from the penance to which offenders had been sentenced by other Bishops. Heito, of Basel, about the year 820, orders that penitents who wish to visit the A.D. 820 Apostolic City should first confess their sins at home, "because they are to be bound or loosed by their own bishop or priest and not by a stranger."

Annual Confession on Ash-Wednesday.

Early in the 9th century there was a decided effort to introduce annual confession on Ash-Wednesday. An order was given that the priest should call upon all[1] who were accustomed to confess to him, to renew their confessions on that day and to make three confessions a year.

Theodulph, in prescribing confession annually, names also Ash-Wednesday as the special day for making confessions, and in the year 822 the Statutes of Corbie order a holiday on that day so that the labouring folk may have time to confess.

A.D. 870　By the Rule of Chrodegang of Metz, confession of sins was encouraged: "He who voluntarily confesses his lighter sins shall be visited with lighter censures." And he prescribed that, every day after 'prime,' each member of the house should confess his faults and accept punishment according to his station.

A.D. 900　Grimlaic, in his Rule[2] for monks, orders them to meet in the evening and examine their consciences for all sins committed during the day, and to make confession of them daily to God in prayer with tears and groaning, as confession leads to repentance, and repentance to pardon, but nothing is said as to confession to a priest, penance or absolution.

---

[1] Martene, de antiq. Eccles. Ritibus, Lib. I. cap. VI. Art. 7: Ex duobus antiquis MSS. insignis ecclesiæ Sancti Gatiani Turonensis, ante annos 800, exaratis.

Præmonere debent omnes sacerdotes eos, qui sibi confiteri solent, ut in capite jejunii concurrere incipiant ad renovandam confessionem.

[2] Grimlaic, Reg. Solitariorum, cap. 25, 29 (Migne, CIII. 606, 618).

No. 58. Mala sua præterita cum lacrymis vel gemitu quotidie in oratione Deo confiteri: et de ipsis malis in reliquo emendare.

Ch. XXIX. Nam ex humilitatis virtute compunctio cordis nascitur. De compunctione cordis confessio peccatorum propagatur. De confessione peccatorum pœnitentia generatur. De pœnitentia autem indulgentia peccatorum percipitur.

The monks at that time had adopted the custom of daily chapters or assemblies, in which sinners were expected to confess their faults and accept punishment, and where accusations could be brought against those who did not voluntarily accuse themselves, even as in the congregations the faithful were more or less accustomed to do the same. This answered all the purposes of discipline.

Regino of Pruhm shows us that, in some places, annual confession was assumed to be the rule, for in Episcopal visitations one of the points to be enquired into is whether any one does not come to confession at least once a year, on Ash-Wednesday.

S. Ulric[1], of Augsburg, ordered his priests to invite A.D. 950 their parishioners to confess yearly just before Ash-Wednesday.

In the instruction which Atto of Vercelli framed for his priests, there is no allusion to any necessary duty to hear confessions or to impose penance. The only form he recognizes is public penance for public sins. So in the admonitions which the priest is to give to his flock, there is no mention of encouraging them to private confession, but they are daily to confess their sins to God with sighs and tears.

In the year 942, at the age of 18, Dunstan was made Abbot of Glastonbury[2], which was at that time little more than a renowned seminary. A few secular priests still ministered in its Church, and it was not

---

[1] S. Udalric Augustan. Sermo Synodalis (Migne, cxxxv. 1072—4): feria quarta ante Quadragesimam plebem ad confessionem invitate, et ei, juxta qualitatem delicti, pœnitentiam injungite, non ex corde vestro, sed sicut in Pœnitentiali scriptum est.

[2] Dr Spence, History of the Church of England, Pt. vi. p. 415.

a monastery in the usual acceptation of the term. Monastic life had really ceased in England in those days, and very little regard for religious matters was held by the people. Dunstan, however, was determined to infuse a new life into the Church, and to repair the mischief which long and constant wars had effected among the works of Alfred. The various educational efforts which the great king had made had well nigh died away. The clergy had reverted largely to a state of ignorance and even of worldliness[1]. Dunstan felt that the cause of education was the cause of religion: he was an eminent teacher himself. Owing to the Viking raids on their precious and unprotected treasures, the more prominent monasteries on the Continent as well as in England had declined. And the closing of these religious houses brought with it a crushing out of religious life throughout the nation. In the year 960 Dunstan was appointed A.D. 967 Primate, and about 967, under his powerful influence, King Edgar the Pacific was led to recommend that all polluted with mortal sin should confess to their Bishops on Ash-Wednesday, which he says is a custom observed beyond the seas, and in a body of English Ecclesiastical observances daily confession to God and yearly to the priest is enjoined.

Dunstan[2] did much to revive the influence of the Church, and after preaching most powerful sermons on Ascension Day, he was on the following Sunday called

---

[1] Dr Spence, History of the Church of England, Pt. VI. p. 419.

[2] Lingard, Anglo-Saxon Church, II. 304: In 988 Dunstan had grown very feeble, and the festival of the Ascension in that year was the last day in which he performed the public service in his Cathedral. As soon as the Gospel had been read, he walked in state from the vestry to the pulpit, and preached with unwonted energy on the

to his rest in the year 988. During the reign of Edgar (960—975) 47 monasteries were founded, restored, or recovered from the secular clergy. The monks were governed by a rule modified from that of S. Benedict, and chiefly derived from Fleury. Monks were brought from Fleury and other foreign monasteries to fill the places of the expelled clergy and to serve as examples to the English of the true monastic life. The Canons of Winchester at that time were sunk in luxury and licentiousness, they refused to perform the offices of the Church, and not content with marrying, indulged themselves in the liberty of changing their wives at pleasure.

Ælfric (by some thought to have been Archbishop of A.D. 995 Canterbury), in his Homily for the First Sunday after Easter, applying the miracle of raising Lazarus to the unbinding of the sinner from the eternal punishment, says[1]: "Every sinful man who conceals his sins, lies dead in the sepulchre, but if he confesses his sins owing to his conscience being awakened, then he goes from the sepulchre, as Lazarus did when Christ bade him arise: then shall the teacher unbind him from the eternal punishment, as the Apostles bodily unbound Lazarus." And again, in another place he says: "Let no man be ashamed

Incarnation of the Saviour, the Redemption of men, and the bliss of heaven. Coming back to the altar, he proceeded with the mass till the end of the Pater Noster, when he turned to the people, addressed them a second time, exhorting them to follow their head and leader to the realms of happiness, and pronounced over them the Episcopal benediction. He then gave the kiss of peace and addressing the congregation for the third time, begged of them to remember him, when he was gone: for he felt that his hour was approaching and that he should see them no more in this world....He died the following Sunday at the age of 64 or 65.

[1] Maskell on Absolution, p. 186.

to make known his sins to one teacher, for he who will not in this world confess his sins with true repentance, shall be put to shame before God Almighty and before his hosts of angels and before all men, at the great doom. His shame shall be endless. For no man obtains forgiveness of his sins from God, unless he confess them to some man of God, and by his doom expiate them." Thus Ælfric showed that he believed that confession to man was a *necessary* preliminary to the remission of sins.

Ælfric wrote several Pastoral Epistles[1] which were highly valued by the Anglo-Saxon Church, and he seems only to press confession on penitents when on their death-bed and their last hours are drawing nigh, and then probably only as a preparation for extreme unction.

---

[1] Ælfric's Pastoral Ep. (Thorpe, I. 465) entitled "Quando dividis chrisma"; The sick man ought earnestly to repent his former sins and promise cessation, and he may confess them till his latest breath: and he shall forgive all those men who before had angered him, and pray for forgiveness for them.

CHAPTER IX.

*The approach of the thousandth year from the
Saviour's birth.*

THE nearness[1] of the thousandth year from the
Saviour's birth had raised a general belief that the second
Advent was close at hand : and in truth there was much
which might easily be construed as fulfilling the predicted
signs of the end—wars and rumours of wars, famines and
pestilences, fearful appearances in the heavens, faith
failing from the earth, and love waxing cold. The
Council of Trosley (909), which lamented the decline of
monastic institutions, had urged the nearness of the end
as a motive for reformation. Many donations of the
time to Churches begin with the form "whereas the
end of the world draweth near," and this belief did much
to revive the power and wealth of the clergy, after the
disorders and losses of the century. The minds of men
were called away from the ordinary cares and employ-
ments of life ; even our knowledge of history has suffered

---

[1] Robertson, Christian Church, Vol. II. p. 402.
* Milman, II. 483.

in consequence, since there was little inclination to bestow labour on the chronicling of events, when no posterity was expected to read the records. Some plunged into desperate recklessness of living: an eclipse of the sun or moon was a signal for multitudes to seek a hiding-place in dens and caves of the earth: and crowds of pilgrims flocked to Palestine, where the Saviour was expected to appear for judgment.

A.D. 1016   A.D. 1016—1035. Canute[1] adopted the Christian Faith, and lived up to it in his private life and in the administration of the public affairs of his kingdom, and he helped by his life and work to raise and make the Church of England. In the year 1027[2], when he made his pilgrimage to Rome, he addressed a letter to the people of England in which he made a sort of 'open confession' in these words. "I have vowed to amend my life in all respects and to rule the kingdoms and the people subject to me with justice and clemency, and if, through the intemperance of youth or negligence, I have hitherto exceeded the bounds of justice in any of my acts, I intend by God's aid to make an entire change for the better." He returned from his pilgrimage, having gained certain privileges for future pilgrims and traders of the English nation. He reared a stone Church in Essex in memory of his great victory over Edmund Ironside "as an atonement for his earlier crimes."

The 11th century was specially a period of war and unrest. Energies were spent in conflicts on the battle-field throughout Europe and England. The shameful

---

[1] Dr Spence, Church of England, Pt. VII. p. 22.
[2] Ibid. p. 23 and also Green's Short History of England, p. 62.

lives of the majority of Popes for more than a century past, strife between pope and antipope culminating in 1044 with three persons, each holding the position of Pope among their followers, tended to lessen the authority of the Papal supremacy, and but little religious life existed among the nations, except what might be found nurtured in the monasteries which had been fostered especially in Normandy and England. Civilization began to flourish in the dominion of Duke Richard the Fearless, during the latter half of the 10th century, and change of manners was accompanied by a more active change of faith, and the land where heathendom had fought most stubbornly for life was becoming bound more closely than other lands to the cause of Christianity and the Church. The dignitaries of the Norman Church were placed in the charge of dioceses in England, both by Edward the Confessor, who had been exiled for so many years in Normandy, and afterwards by William, who had gained in war the sovereignty of England. Long trains of penitents, in sackcloth and ashes, paraded through the streets and filled the Churches with their litanies, when any special trouble seemed to demand prayers for the mercy of the Almighty. These however had been driven into the class of penitents owing to their having committed some well-known act of sin, rather than becoming so in consequence of having made confession of a sin, which otherwise would have remained concealed. Henry III., Emperor of Germany, exercised great authority over the affairs of the Church, and seems to have been bent on crushing out simony and in freeing the Pope from the tyranny of Italian nobles. He was in the height of his power in the middle of the 11th century, and it is said that he so greatly felt the responsibilities of his powerful position in the world, that he never put on his regal insignia without having first confessed, and undergone the discipline in satisfaction of his sins.

A.D. 1060 Peter Damiani[1] describes the dowager Empress Agnes, widow of Henry III. of Germany, on her visit to Rome, confessing to him all her sins since she was five years old. He tells us also that the Empress grew more anxious as to her soul, as she drew near her end. Her latter years were passed in the strictest ascetic observances, confessing daily not only her acts but her thoughts and even her dreams, and performing religiously whatever penance was assigned to her. As the Popes of this period required that all who were ranked as penitents should abandon all occupations in court, camp or trade, most persons were inclined to defer their confessions of sin until they were drawing near to their life's end, as reconciliation was to involve their giving up all that made life attractive to them. Peter Damiani tells us that the monks, when assembled in their daily or weekly chapters, were expected to confess their faults, or to be accused, whereupon immediate punishment usually of scourging was inflicted, and consisted of from 20 to 40 stripes for each fault confessed or proved against them. He[2] too recommended voluntary flagellation, as a sort of purgatory. He thought it well thus to punish

---

[1] Dr Lea, Confession, Vol. I. p. 196.

[*] Peter Damiani, Opusc. LVI. cap. 5.

[2] Peter Damiani, Opusc. XLIII.: De laude flagellorum. Non opus est, Domine, ut officio tuo me puniri præcipias, non expedit, ut ipse me justi examinis vitiose percellas: ipse mihi manus injicio, ipse de me vindictam capio, vicemque meis peccatis reddo.

ourselves for our sins: if men were allowed to redeem their sins with money surely those, who have no money, ought to have some means of redemption provided for them.

In the Cluniac Order, which was more rigid than A.D. 1080 the Benedictine, the only command for secret confession was that the novice, when received, confessed all the sins committed in secular life; and the monk, when dying, confessed again, as a preparation for extreme unction. There were considerable variations in the Service Books[1] in the different dioceses of England, but that of Sarum, issued in 1085, gradually superseded the others. At the commencement of the Eucharistic Service in the uses of Sarum, Bangor, York and Hereford, we find that priest and people confessed to one another openly before the congregation and to God in the following form: " 'Confiteor etc.' I confess to God, to the Blessed Mary, to all saints and to you. I have sinned too much in thought, word and deed, my blame. I pray the Blessed Mary, all the saints of God, and you to pray for me." To which is replied " The Almighty God have mercy on thee, and forgive thee all thy sins, deliver thee of all evil, save and confirm thee in every good work, and lead thee to everlasting life."

In place of this we have, in our present Service Book, the very solemn and hearty General Confession at the commencement of our Service for communicants.

Lanfranc[2], who was Archbishop of Canterbury from A.D. 1090

[1] W. Maskell, The Ancient Liturgy of the Church of England, p. 14.

[2] Lanfranc, Sermo sive Sententiæ: Octavum est, ut puram confessionem de omnibus peccatis suis faciant, quam tamen confessionem non passim omnibus, prout cui libuerit, nisi tantummodo suis Prælatis, vel quibus iidem Prælati potestatem tribuunt, faciant.

to 1080, is known to have recommended private confession as a wholesome custom.

While William Rufus[1] lay sick at Gloucester it seemed for the first time as though the old pagan spirit of the ancestors of the Red King failed him, and he turned, dying as he fancied himself to be, to the consolations of the religion he had so long flouted. In all haste, the holy Anselm, who had the greatest reputation of all in his time for that higher knowledge of soul-healing, was sent for. The king confessed his many sins and promised to do all by way of reparation that Anselm required, pledging himself if his life were spared in the words of the English Chronicle "to correct his life, to sell no more Churches nor to let them out to farm, but to defend them by his kingly power, to take away un-
righteous laws and to establish righteous ones." Anselm[2] writes to his brother Burgundius who was about to depart on a pilgrimage to the Holy Land, neither to take his sins with him, nor to leave them behind him, but to make confession of them all since infancy.

In the same year Urban II., in preaching on behalf of the Crusades, insisted on the easiness of the remedy for sin, and even proposed the relaxation of all penance in favour of those who should assume the Cross. A cardinal pronounced a confession of sins in the name

[1] Dean Spence, Church of England, Pt. VIII. p. 155.

W. Hunt, English Church in the Middle Ages, p. 90.

[2] S. Anselm, Epist. Lib. III. Ep. 66: Consulo et precor, ut si hanc viam (ire Hierosolymam) faciatis, nec vobiscum peccata quæ fecistis, portetis, nec domi peccatum relinquatis: et ut deinceps voluntatem bene vivendi sicut verus Christianus vestri ordinis habeatis. Facite confessionem omnium peccatorum vestrorum nominatim ab infantia vestra, quantum recordari potestis.

of all who were to share in the expedition, and the Pope bestowed his absolution on them. Almost incredible were the spiritual promises[1] which Pope Urban dared authoritatively to make. He offered absolution for all sins, there was no crime which might not be redeemed by joining the crusading force, absolution without penance to all who would take up arms in this sacred cause.

The synod of Gran[2] enjoins three confessions a year, A.D. 1099 at Easter, Pentecost and at Christmas.

The form of penance, severe and of long duration, though regulated by the nature of the sins according to the Penitentials which from time to time were issued by persons in high authority in the Church, came by degrees to consist in fasting or prayer or alms or other spiritual acts, and in the 11th century included service on a Crusade. This penance had to continue for a certain definite time, unless the authority, by which it was imposed, granted an indulgence. It was assumed that the sinner either directly or indirectly confessed his sin. This gradually took the place of the old public penance, and undoubtedly led the way to the later confessional. The performance of the penance imposed or taken up was the *chief* element, and the act of reconciliation or of absolution imperfectly existed.

---

[1] Dean Spence, History of the Church of England, Pt. IX. p. 178.
[2] Dr Lea on Confession, Vol. I. p. 196.
  * Synod. Strigonens. II.

Confession when death seems to be near.

A.D. 1115   Peter de Honestis[1] drew up an elaborate account of monastic discipline, including baths and blood-letting, but the only provision for private confession is on the death-bed, where the dying brother unburdens his soul to the prior or to priests deputed for the purpose, after which he receives absolution from the whole body of the brethren.

A.D. 1128   Abbot Guigo has left on record rules of the Carthusian Order, wherein the monks are ordered to shave six times a year, and let blood five times, but the only allusion to confession is on the death-bed, when the dying monk is expected to confess to a priest, and receive absolution.

Public confession in their Chapters still continued to be made, although this had quite died out with the laity, and the Church endeavoured to render private confession popular as the best substitute. But at this time religious energy was more engaged in increasing monasteries than in providing more of the regular clergy, and with the scanty supply of priests it would

---

[1] Peter de Honestis, Regulæ Clericor. Lib. II. cap. 22 (Migne, CLXIII.): Illi ergo si febrem continuare, vel languorem increscere persenserint, tunc advocato priore, seu præposito et presbyteris, ad hoc officium deputatis, plenam de peccatis suis confessionem faciant, sicque præmissa de præteritis culpis secundum prioris jussum satisfactione, et in futuro sui emendatione, susceptaque ab omni conventu benedictione, et peccatorum absolutione, fideliter per eos, quibus injunctum est, custodiantur, ut eos in cunctis necessitatibus suis ministros aptissimos habeant: qui semel saltem in die cum visitantibus se fratribus confessionem faciant, atque orationis benedictionem ab eis exquirant.

have been impossible for people to have made frequent confessions.

A passage in Honorius of Autun throws light on the A.D. 1130 manner[1] in which auricular was gradually supplanting public confession, and the confusion still existing between the old and the new. The memory of public confession was preserved in the ritual, wherein the congregation and the priest made a general confession of sins—a specific admission, on the part of all joining in it, of having polluted themselves with each and every mortal sin recited in it, and on its conclusion the priest administered absolution in the only form as yet known to the Church, by praying for it.

About the middle of the 12th century Peter Lombard[2] repeats the Carthaginian Canon, which prohibited the priest from granting reconciliation, except in cases of necessity, without consulting the Bishop, and makes no attempt to harmonize this with the existing earnest effort to render confession universal and frequent, and to bring every one under control of the parish priest.

Tracy[3], one of the four knights who murdered Thomas A.D. 1170 à Becket in Canterbury Cathedral, some long time afterwards is reported to have made a confession to the Bishop of Exeter, and said that their spirits, after the murder was done, failed them and they retired at once with

---

[1] Dr Lea on Confession, Vol. I. p. 206.

* Honorii Augustod. Speculum Ecclesiæ. De nativitate Domini.

[2] Peter Lombardi Lib. IV. Dist. XX. § 6: Non debet tamen presbyter pœnitentem reconciliare inconsulto episcopo, nisi ultima necessitas cogat. Unde in Carthaginensi concilio 26, q. 6, Presbyter, inconsulto episcopo, non reconciliet pœnitentem, nisi absente episcopo vel ultima necessitas cogat.

[3] Dean Spence, Church of England, Pt. IX. p. 202.

trembling steps, expecting the earth to open and swallow them up.

It is difficult to understand how the matter of this confession was divulged by the Bishop, unless the confession partook of the nature of an open one rather than a secret one.

CHAPTER X.

THE system of penance became more and more widely different from what it had originally been. Most especially[1] the Penitential discipline suffered from a system which now superseded the penitential books of earlier times, the system of Indulgences which were granted by way of inducement to perform some service for the Church. These, unlike the indulgences of former days, were not limited to the forgiveness of particular sins, but extended to all. This system was brought into its fullest operation by the Crusades, from the time when Urban II. at Clermont proclaimed a plenary indulgence for all who should share in the Holy War. These indulgences indeed were intended as remissions of those temporal penalties only, which it was believed that the sinner must undergo, either in this life or in purgatory: but the people in general understood them, and persisted in doing so, as promises of eternal forgiveness, while they overlooked any condition of repentance or charity which had been annexed to them. This is proved by the conduct of the Crusaders and of the Latins in the Holy Land.

---

[1] Robertson, History of the Christian Church, Vol. III. p. 270.
* Planck, IV. ii. 396, 398, 402, 403.

At the close of the 12th century, Peter Cantor[1] asserts that "the more the priests, to whom confession is made, the speedier is the pardon," and this must have been no uncommon proceeding. In 978, Otho II. confessed to Pope Benedict VII. and a number of bishops and priests: in 1089, William Rufus not only made his confession to the holy Anselm, but he also summoned several priests to hear his dying confession: in 1135, Henry I. confessed to his chaplains and then to Archbishop Hugo: in 1199, Richard I., dying before the Castle of Châlus, had three Cistercian Abbots to hear his confession. This was probably done from a feeling of shame, that the knowledge of him, confessing, might be divided, rather than that his sins should all be confided to one.

The question, whether confession to a priest were necessary in order to forgiveness of sin, was often discussed. Gratian and Peter Lombard give the arguments on each side: Gratian[2] (A.D. 1152), with some qualification, decides against the necessity, though some affirm that he adds "upon what authorities and upon what strength of reasons both these opinions are grounded, I have briefly declared; which of them we should rather cleave to is left to the judgment of the reader, for both have their favourers, wise and religious men." Peter

A.D. 1152

---

[1] Dr Lea, Confession, Vol. I. p. 354.

* P. Cantor Verb. abbreviat. cap. 143.

[2] Gratian, Pars II. causa XXXIII. qu. 3, dist. 1 (Migne, CLXXXVII.): Utrum sola cordis contritione, et secreta satisfactione, absque oris confessione quisque possit Deo satisfacere, redeamus. Sunt enim qui dicunt quemlibet criminis veniam sine confessione facta ecclesiæ et sacerdotali judicio posse promereri......

Lombard[1] holds that there is this necessity. He teaches that true repentance must consist of three parts—the compunction of the heart, the confession of the mouth and the satisfaction of work, but he holds that if the assistance of a priest cannot be had, confession to a lay Christian is allowable. As to the effect of priestly absolution, he holds that the priest cannot forgive sins, but can only declare them to be remitted or retained: that although he may have been forgiven by God, yet absolution by the priest's judgment is necessary in the face of the Church: but that this absolution is valid in so far only as it agrees with the Divine judgment.

Richard of S. Victor, though he sneers at this opinion, did not venture to maintain that the priest had absolute power to forgive as with God's authority: and as yet the form of absolution continued to be in the form of a prayer and not as the sentence of a judge.

Towards the close of the 12th century the Rules[2] of S. Jacques de Montfort have no provision for

---

[1] Peter Lombard, Sent. Lib. IV. distinc. XVII. (Migne, CXCII.): Illa confessio nos liberat, quæ fit cum pœnitentia. Pœnitentia vera est dolor cordis, et amaritudo animæ pro malis, quæ quisque commisit. Tanta itaque vis confessionis est, ut si deest sacerdos confiteatur proximo. Sæpe enim contingit quod pœnitens non potest verecundari coram sacerdote, quem desideranti nec tempus, nec locus offert. Etsi ille cui confitebitur potestatem non habeat solvendi, fit tamen dignus venia ex sacerdotis desiderio, qui crimen confitetur socio...

Ostensum est ex parte qualiter sacerdotes dimittant peccata vel teneant, et tamen retinuit sibi Deus quamdam singularem potestatem dimittendi vel retinendi, quia ipse solus per se debitum æternæ mortis solvit, et animam interius purgat.

[2] Dr Lea, Confession, Vol. I. p. 200 and following.

* Antiquæ consuetu. Canon. Regulæ, c. 4—7. Martene, Thesaur. IV. 1218—1220.

auricular confession, but the public confession and accusation in the daily chapters are in full force, when the prior grants absolution and adjudges the penance or punishment.

The Rules of monastic life have been collected in "usus antiquiores Ordinis Cisterciensis," and chapters 70, 75 and 94 provide for accusation and self-accusation in their daily assemblies, followed by punishment and absolution, and there is no injunction of private confession, though the Abbot, Prior and sub-Prior are empowered to listen to those who desire to confess even very trivial things. Even when on the death-bed, no formal confession is prescribed. The dying man merely said 'Confiteor' or 'Mea culpa,' 'I pray you to pray for me, for all my sins,' and the absolution was equally informal. The sacramental character of penitence was taking shape, and from sermons of S. Bernard not long after, we find that confession and communion at Easter were becoming necessary.

A.D. 1202   Innocent III. made some changes in the Rule of the Order of Grammont, and from this we learn that it represents a period during which the sacramental character of penitence was acknowledged and confession was becoming increasingly important.

The monastic regulations concerning confession during the 12th century throw much light upon the transition from the ancient custom of public confession in the congregation to the innovation of auricular confession. To the monk his daily or weekly chapter represented the congregation of the Early Church, and in this he was bound to make confession of his sins: if he failed to do so, he could be accused by any one cognizant of his offence, and in the later period the office of circatores (spies) was devised to aid in enforcing the discipline of the Rule.

Penance was soon to be regarded as a Sacrament, the time of doing penance was reduced to the time of making an exact confession of sins and the receiving the priestly absolution, which now took the form of an authoritative pronouncement, "I absolve thee from thy sins."

When Hildebrand was raised to the pontifical chair at Rome, the interference of the Popes commenced in the administration of the civil power, which extended to the investiture of Bishops of the Church, in the various countries of Europe. Hildebrand was created Pope under the title of Gregory VII.: he raised the Papacy from the degradation into which it had fallen for many years. He seemed to rule over the greater part of Europe. During the twelve years he held this exalted position, from 1073 to 1085, he worked a marvellous change by his determined will and superior abilities in the influence and control, which the Roman Pontiff was to hold over the kingdoms of the world. He threatened Philip I. of France with excommunication, and carried this power into execution against Henry IV. of Germany, whom he treated with barbarous cruelty. He used every means to establish the hierarchy over surrounding nations, and in doing so he disregarded all the ordinary claims of justice, truth and mercy. Urban II. (1088—1099) was firm, active, and enterprising, and his artfulness and caution gave him more success in dominating over others than the undisguised audacity and assumption of Gregory had gained. He deluded the people to join in the Crusade by promises of complete absolution of their sins, of which they made no confession. Eugenius III. (1145—1153) did much to elevate the power of his position by promoting the second Crusade, and making similar promises to those of Urban with respect to the absolution of sins, for those who joined in the Holy War. He however had somewhat troublous times through favouring the French rather than the Roman clergy. Popes followed one another in quick succession until Innocent III. who held the Papacy from 1198 to 1216. During this period he laid England under an Interdict, owing to the resistance of John, King of England, to the Pope's power. This Pope "was dreaded by all, above all the popes, who for many years had gone before him." He had carried out with a high hand in every country in Western Europe his policy of establishing the papal authority over all kings, princes and rulers of the nations.

A.D. 1215 In the last year of his Papacy he held the Fourth Lateran Council, A.D. 1215, where there was a vast assemblage of 2283 persons of high authority in Church and State. Arrangements were made for another Crusade to the East, to be carried out in the following year.

The two most important Canons[1] which were adopted related to doctrine and to discipline. The 1st, which for the first time laid down, by the authority of the whole Western Church, the doctrine of transubstantiation in the Eucharist; and the 21st, which prescribed for every Catholic Christian the duty of confessing once a year at least to his own priest, and of yearly receiving the Holy Eucharist at Easter.

[1] Robertson, History of the Christian Church, Vol. III. p. 377.

The necessity of secret confession was imposed in these terms[1]: "That everyone of either sex, as soon as he has arrived at years of discretion, should confess at least once a year to his own priest, and endeavour to accomplish according to his strength the Penance imposed on him."

During the whole of the century, after the publication of this Canon, frequent allusion is made, whenever clergy and laity met for the discussion of Church matters, to the new duties required of the Parish Priests and of the people. Arrangements are made by the authorities of the Church for enforcing this new Rule, and disastrous penalties are threatened for those neglecting it.

In these terms 'Auricular Confession' was established. Concerning this Canon we may join with the learned Hooker and say[2]: "That to frustrate Men's Confession and consideration of sin, except every circumstance which may aggravate the same, be unript and laid in the balance is a merciless extremity: although it be true, that as near as we can, such wounds must be searched to the very bottom. Last of all, to set down the like stint, and to shut up the door of mercy against Penitents, which come short thereof in the devotion of their prayers, in the continuance of their Fasts: in the largeness and bounty of their Alms, or in the course of any other such like Duties, is more

---

[1] Fourth Council of Lateran, c. 21: Omnis utriusque sexus fidelis, postquam ad annos discretionis pervenerit, omnia sua solus peccata confiteatur fideliter (saltem semel in anno) proprio Sacerdoti, et injunctam sibi Pœnitentiam studeat pro viribus adimplere.

[2] Hooker, Eccles. Pol. bk. VI. pp. 104, 105.

than God Himself hath thought meet and consequently more than mortal men should presume to do."

General Summary.

From the foregoing we gather that in the early days of the Church—in the time of the Apostles—the confessions that we read about had special reference to those persons who, having hitherto lived without any faith in Christ or following after His example of love to God and to man, on their conscience being awakened, confessed their former ignorance, and declared that they were desirous to embrace the Christian Religion. The early Christians consulted together for their mutual benefit, and especially when the hand of sickness or death was upon them they sought the sympathy and consolation of others, to whom they opened up their hearts and gave expression to such faults of their former life as weighed upon their consciences, and troubled them, especially at a time which appeared to them to be their last hours on earth. As time advanced and the number of those who were enrolled as members of Christ's Church rapidly grew, it became necessary to preserve as much as possible the good name of the community, and if any member incurred the guilt of infidelity, impurity or blood-guiltiness, he was shut out from all privileges until he had confessed, publicly before his congregation, his sin, and had given visible proofs of his repentance and amendment. For the first 250 years the Bishop, as the chief pastor in each diocese, managed the whole matter of the confession before the congregation, the special prayers and services, the course of humiliation and penance to be gone through by a penitent sinner. And S. Cyprian specially complains that those who had lapsed and offered sacrifices to idols during the Decian persecution had been readmitted by those who had no authority, and ignored the fact that the Bishop alone had the power. Owing to the inconveniences and scandal that might arise from open confessions in the Church, it was found desirable to appoint in each Diocese a penitentiary priest, to whom the sinner should resort and make a preliminary confession, whereupon he should advise what should be confessed openly before the congregation and what had better be kept back. S. Anthony, who lived from the middle of the 3rd century to the middle of the 4th, seems to have been one of the first to advocate private confession, but this was among his monks, whom he directs to write down their thoughts, and communicate them to one another, but this could not give colour to priestly confession, as the monks were not clerics. However, after the year 500 the Office of Penitentiary was abolished, owing to a sad misdirection in a very important and scandalous case. From this time the whole management of penitents reverted to the Bishops.

The Fathers, when writing on the subject of Repentance, never press Auricular Confession as a necessity for repentance, but nevertheless speak of the comfort which penitents may obtain by seeking the counsel of one entrusted with the oracles of God, and unburdening their minds to him of the sin which is causing them so much disquietude. The same Fathers acknowledge only

R.

three sorts of Repentance, one for all manner of sins previous to Baptism—the second, daily for the lesser sins of life—and the third, which took the form of public penance for any particular sin of a gross character that may have been committed. Although it was generally agreed that if a sinner again fell into gross sin after having made public confession and received absolution, he could not a second time be admitted to Penance, yet he was not to be regarded as shut out from salvation, but might obtain it without the use of confession. During the time the Office of Penitentiary was maintained, the penitent would perform private penance for such great sins as it was thought undesirable to confess publicly, and thus public penance was gradually displaced by that which was wholly of a private character. For the first four centuries those guilty of any one of the three great branches of crimes, heresy, murder or unchastity, were required to make open confession before the brethren, either voluntary or after accusation, and then undergo the penance imposed before they could be reconciled to the Church. If also any sinner was troubled at having committed any lesser sin, he was directed to make confession to God in his daily prayer and ask His forgiveness, which he would most certainly obtain. But beyond doubt there was no attempt made to insist upon periodical confession as necessary when the conscience was not troubled or weighed down by some definite sin. About the middle of the 5th century sinners' feelings were so much regarded that they were allowed to make out their public confessions in writing, which were read out by an officer of the Church to the congregation, but this was so far disapproved by Pope

Leo that he refused to allow the practice, and further
he required that in future sins confessed privately to the
priest should not be published at all in the Church.
Public confession of sins was the only form recognized
as yet, but Leo's direction soon led to its discontinuance,
though public penance for great sins was still performed.
By the beginning of the 7th century both public confession and public penance seem almost to have died out,
and the General Form of Confession was established as
the rule.

Towards the end of the 8th century the introduction
of periodical confession as a preparation for Christmas
Communion was advocated as if there was a necessity
for some cleansing of the conscience, though it had not
felt any burden of its sin. The Penitential Books, which
provided all the details of the sins of a lifetime, prove
that voluntary confession had scarcely gained a hold upon
the people. By the 9th century private confession and
its natural accompaniment private penance became some-
what common. The sins, which were to be examined
into, were described under eight heads in the place of
the original three, and confessions began to be imposed
immediately before the great Lenten Fast.

The Archbishop of Canterbury, if Ælfric were really
Archbishop, at the end of the 1000th year, in plain terms
declared that confession to man was necessary in order
to obtain remission of sins. Then came a time when
religious observances waned before the ravages of war
and the uneasiness which then prevailed. The fears of
the people were sadly worked upon, and confession before
death became a rule before the dying man could receive
the Holy Communion, which he was taught to regard

as a 'viaticum' to heaven. The power of the Parish
Priest over the people of his cure grew to be excessive.
Towards the middle of the 12th century Gratian tells
us that many learned men joined in the controversy,
whether it was sufficient to confess to God only or
whether it was necessary to confess to the Priest also,
but he fails to give any decision.   Innocent III., however, determines that a Rule of the Church must be
established on the point, and calls the Fourth Lateran
Council together, A.D. 1215, and makes the Rule absolute for all those who desire to be regarded as faithful
members of the Church, and by this Council the Doctrine
of Auricular Confession was established.